Ros Wilson's
Talk Write

Talk:Write

Written by Ros Wilson.
Edited and proof read by Richard Robinson.
Cover and design by Dan Wilson.

Published by P and R Education Ltd.
83 Haigh Lane, Haigh, Wakefield, West Yorkshire, S75 4DA.
Directors – Ben Pilmer and Richard Robinson.

www.RosWilsonEd.com
hello@RosWilsonEd.com
Twitter: @RosBigWriting

ISBN: 978-1-8381761-1-2.

First Published in 2021. First Edition.

About Ros

Ros entered the teaching profession in 1965 and has served continuously since. She has wide experience in education, including: working with pupils with SEND; working with pupils with EAL; senior leadership; head of a large primary department overseas; school start-up; local authority advisor; primary strategy manager; independent consultant; advanced skills teacher (AST) assessor; Ofsted inspector; creator and published author of Big Writing and associated texts (Oxford University Press). Ros recently published a book for early career teachers: *It Takes 5 Years to Become a Teacher* (2021).

Ros has a Certificate of Education from Leeds University (1965), a Diploma of Higher Education from London University (1979), and a Master of Education (specialised in assessment) from Leeds University (1994). She is currently proud to be a governor in a school located in an area of severe socio-economic deprivation.

Get in Touch

Send Ros an email
hello@RosWilsonEd.com

Follow Ros on Twitter for fun and interesting discussions
@RosBigWriting

Feedback for Talk:Write

Beth Bennet

Recently retired teacher / SENDCo / DHT

Talk:Write is coherent and systematically develops what many schools already do, so would only need a few practical tweaks to the timetable to embed it into daily practice.

From the point of view of a class teacher, it is very clear what needs to be done, when and how, as well as how it joins up with the writing sessions each week. The format also allows for individual classes/schools to slot in whatever subject specific vocabulary they need to.

The 10 to 15-minute sessions a day would be easy to plan and deliver. The activities are well thought out and could also be used in those spare few minutes you sometimes get in class.

The videos, and ability to revisit them, offer teachers and teaching assistants ongoing support.

The EAL section is incredibly useful and supportive for NQTs, ECTs, and any who have not had experience of teaching EAL children.

The whole approach lends itself particularly well to teaching children with SEND, as the regular, short sessions will support them systematically to introduce, revisit, and retain vocabulary much more than longer, less focused lessons. The format could also be used in interventions and small group/individual pre and post teaching activities to support those who need more than a single session a day.

Simon Blower

Co-Founder, Pobble

The Pobble team have always been huge admirers of Ros and her brilliant work. We have been fortunate to work with her over the last few years and always take great ideas away from our discussions and her fantastic presentations. As teachers passionate about helping children to become better writers, we are delighted to see Ros sharing some more of her brilliant ideas in this new book and are proud to see Pobble 365 featured as a recommended resource.

Chris Dyson

Headteacher of Parklands Primary School

In Talk:Write, Ros Wilson successfully sets out a model to enhance the teaching of writing. The book can be used as part of enriching CPD which can be tailored to the needs of the school.

Ros's principal is based on the understanding that talk is key to writing. She uses inclusive strategies whereby children will be proud of their difference and dialects, whilst developing their use of Standard English.

In Talk:Write, Ros effectively breaks down the process of writing into clear and explicit strategies. There is an awareness of real life experiences of 'local speak' and home experience of language. This is valued with practical, positive, and playful suggestions which encourage family involvement.

This book is the writing CPD we have all been waiting for. It is warm, fun, real, and exciting. As a reader you are left chomping at the bit to incorporate the process into your school.

Ben Harding

Independent Education Consultant, Creator of WWNumbers

Much has changed in the world of education, and in the world, since Ros Wilson took the UK by storm in the mid-2000s with her approach to teaching and assessing writing in primary schools. And her work is not yet complete, both in terms of the nation's continuing desperate need for young children to acquire an essential oral basis for effective written communication, and in terms of Ros's immense offering to those teachers that are on the hunt for unlocking the secrets of how to teach writing with a depth that provides a lasting impact.

Talk:Write is a comprehensive, cohesive, and contemporary structure. It provides a school, and/or a teacher, with a serious strategy for doing the fun little things each day that add up to make the biggest of educational differences. It is a treasure chest of pedagogical content knowledge to lean on and learn from.

Simon Kidwell

Principal, Trade Union Official

This book reinforces that crucial link between talking and writing and the need to train children to develop agility with their use of language. I grew up in a region where the local dialect was strongly embedded across family life and the local community, and as a young person I often found the process of switching between the spoken word and writing in Standard English a slow and taxing experience. Ros's approach gives teachers the tools to teach children how to 'code switch' through the teaching of 'suave speak', whilst still valuing and celebrating the local dialects that enrich our school communities.

Julie Lilly

Headteacher (retired), Manager of Beyond Levels CPD

I had the great honour of having an early peek at this book before it was published. With its linked online CPD videos, it provides a complete toolkit for raising the standards of children's verbal and written communication across your school, or in your individual classroom. Just one of the Talk:Write elements is the five codes of speech, which exemplifies the teaching of Standard English, not by 'teaching children to *talk posh* through elocution-type lessons', but from within a framework that explores, respects, and celebrates each child's own speech.

This book is jam-packed with practical suggestions for the busy teacher from someone steeped in the subject – Ros Wilson.

Enjoy!

Professor Dame Alison Peacock

Chief Executive of the Chartered College of Teaching

Packed full of advice and practical examples, this book shows how teachers can develop children's vocabulary. We see the importance of becoming a fluent talker whilst learning to write. I love the idea of 'suave' words and language use. Highly recommended for all those seeking to value heritage and local languages whilst embedding the necessary skills of Standard English.

Kirstie Pilmer

Teacher, Upton Primary School

This book came just at the right time for me. My class had many grammar and spelling issues, mainly due to their broad South Yorkshire accents. Most of their sentences began with 'so' and it was not uncommon to find words like 'cos' in their work (one boy genuinely didn't know the word should be because).

I had a small window of time to implement Talk:Write (because I was due to go on maternity leave), but I was astonished with the results. It gave the children an opportunity to articulate their sentences while giving me the chance to correct any grammar issues. As a class, we also 'suaved up' each other's sentences. I found that this was not just useful for the child who had offered the sentence, but for other children who didn't have many ideas of their own. Talk:Write started to happen naturally across all subject areas. I encouraged the children to correct my deliberate grammar and spelling mistakes in the classroom and I welcomed any offers to 'suave up' my own vocabulary. Staff even found my children telling them to 'suave speak' when they came in our classroom! Discussion on how they could do this in a polite and respectful way became a priority!

Having seen the impact Talk:Write had on my class in such a short amount of time, I will most definitely be using it in my teaching moving forward.

Jez Smith

Lead Professional for English, Discovery Schools Trust

Talk is the foundation of successful learning and Ros Wilson does an amazing job of providing teachers with the necessary strategies to maximise pupils' oracy skills. Through the various Talk:Write strategies explored, teachers and pupils will be equipped with effective and engaging tools; empowered to make the best of their 'voice'; and enabled to produce successful written outcomes across the primary curriculum.

With the art of conversation being in danger of becoming lost, Wilson's Talk:Write is a much-needed programme. This book (and its associated online material) is a practical resource packed with useful activities, games, and ideas for developing pupils' oracy and writing skills.

Dawn Titus

Headteacher, St Joseph's Primary School

Since launching Talk:Write at St Joseph's, we have seen an improved stamina for writing with the children. We initially completed the four-week introductory narrative sessions and thought that the pupils might find it repetitive spreading a narrative over the four weeks. It was in fact the opposite.

The pupils really looked forward to the Talk:Write sessions every week so that they could continue their stories. They had time to think and talk to each other as well as family members at home about what could happen next in their stories.

The use of question words for each stage of writing gave the pupils a focus and led to more detailed writing. Teachers had to make sure that pupils read back through what they had previously written so that there was continuity, but this was a skill that we were trying to build up with pupils across the curriculum.

Another aspect of Talk:Write which has worked very well with pupils across the school is the introduction of the whole school 'suave' word. We have introduced a word a week to the pupils in class, as well as the parents via text message and on the website. The pupils have enjoyed the method of learning the spelling of the word by writing with their finger on different surfaces. Adults both at school and parents (as heard by staff in the playground) have been using these words in context with the children and the effect of this has been the children using the words in their writing across the curriculum and in context.

Emma Turner

Research and CPD Lead, Discovery Schools Trust

This resource is quite simply staggering. Pulling together decades' of knowledge, experience, and wisdom, it is a one stop shop for anyone who wishes to develop their practice. Supportive, accessible, rooted in excellence, and full of gems from the very first to the final words. From NQTs to experienced leaders within English, this is sure to be an instant indispensable classic – a book to make us wonder how we ever managed without it.

Contents

For video CPD, resources, and updates, visit our website:

www.RosWilsonEd.com

Foreword

Professor Sam Twiselton, OBE

'Reading and writing floats on a sea of talk' (Britton, 1970) is a term I have used throughout my career and it neatly captures the philosophy of this book.

It is, however, a philosophy that goes further and deeper than a few words can portray. As this book so powerfully demonstrates, language and communication are at the core of intellectual and personal development. Words, thoughts, and concepts are so deeply interconnected that I would argue that talk is the foundation of learning. What I love about this book is that it takes this deeply philosophical, abstract foundation and turns it into concrete practical ways that help teachers and schools to address the implications that arise from it.

Teachers need to help all children to develop their talk so that from this they can develop everything else. It is the foundation and therefore supremely important. Too often it can be overlooked, without recognising the importance of thinking deeply about and planning for it. The approaches taken in this book to address this are clear, structured, and completely actionable in classroom practice. This matters for all children but matters most for those who have had less rich language experiences outside of school. As some of the data shows, the gap for these children gets wider and wider at alarming rates if these deficits are not addressed.

The many advisory roles I have taken on (from the Carter Review of ITT to Teacher Recruitment and Retention, the ITT Core Content Framework, the Specialist NPQs to the Market Review of ITT) all have teacher development at their heart. This in turn needs to have talk as the foundation of learning at its heart. This was the clear message from the All Party Parliamentary Group special enquiry on oracy teacher development round table I recently chaired. This book will be enormously helpful in supporting this cause.

Professor Samantha Twiselton is the Director of Sheffield Institute of Education at Sheffield Hallam University, Vice President (External) of the Chartered College of Teaching, and Deputy Chair of Opportunity Area Partnership Board. Follow Sam on Twitter: @samtwiselton

Introduction

I qualified as a teacher in 1965 and started my career in a large secondary modern school in an area of considerable deprivation in West Yorkshire. Since then, I have taught pupils aged 4 to 16 in every year from year 1 to year 11. The majority of schools I have worked in have had significant challenges of different complexities, from primary schools through middle schools and secondary schools, many with a diverse range of ethnicities and cultures and a constant turn-over of families and pupils; from small-island, isolated community schools with few resources and sometimes impoverished and unsafe facilities, to large, fee-paying, English curriculum schools overseas. I have lived and taught overseas for a total of 19 years and have continued to work as a consultant in both UK and overseas settings for a further 20 years.

From 1992 to 1999, I was proud to work as the primary advisor for assessment in Kirklees Local Authority. I qualified as an Ofsted inspector and participated in both authority and national school inspections. In 2001, I established an independent education consultancy, specialising primarily in raising standards in writing for pupils aged 5 to 13. I qualified and practised as an assessor of advanced skills teachers (ASTs) and continued to contribute to Ofsted inspections. For three years, I was contracted to a large, urban education authority in West Yorkshire as primary strategy manager.

In 1999, I had the great privilege of being approached to co-open a large English curriculum school from scratch with a valued former colleague who had been appointed principal. Located in an isolated community established to house the employees of two major off-shore gas companies in Qatar, it was my responsibility to lead the primary school for children aged 4 to 11 in six blocks of apartments, while my colleague worked to establish the secondary school and the creation of a purpose-built school for all.

Of the opening cohort of 450 pupils, only 10 were able to speak English and many had received limited previous education in their home countries of the Middle and Far East. Pupils were of all abilities, and many were from impoverished backgrounds, their parents being employed to work as labourers by the companies. By the close of the first year, there were 45 languages in the school and over 60 in the second year. The numbers on roll increased constantly throughout every academic year.

In May 2001, the pupils who had started school aged 9 to 10 (in year five, 1999 to 2000) took the year six May SAT tests at age 11. 100 percent of pupils achieved the English expectation for 11-year-olds after only two years of learning English. In England, 75 percent of pupils in primary schools achieved the national expectation that year and – in addition – a percentage of pupils in English primary schools were exempt from the tests, which none of ours were.

For 20 years, I have worked nationally and internationally to raise standards in English for pupils of all ages and abilities. I have published nine books addressing a range of aspects of education, including the teaching of writing, talk, the creative curriculum, and assessment. I have supported schools on four continents and in over 20 countries.

Implementing Continuing Professional Development (CPD) in Schools

Devising new programmes and systems for improvements to the quality of education in schools is an extremely responsible and skilled task. It requires the creator to have proven knowledge and expertise in the area of education that the programme addresses, as well as a thorough understanding of how schools are managed and run, and how new initiatives are introduced and embedded.

In writing about the variable quality of CPD experienced in schools, Tom Sherrington (education consultant, author of The Learning Rainforest, teacher trainer) listed the main issues that could prove barriers or inhibitors to schools benefiting from professional development.

He said:

> "
>
> There are various complexities and competing tensions and only so much time:
> - Alignment with whole school priorities vs. specific needs and interests of individual teachers.
> - Short-term improvement vs. longer-term development.
> - Generic common practice vs. specific curriculum issues.
> - Experienced/expert teachers vs. teachers needing structure and support.
> - Building on internal expertise vs. drawing on external expertise.
> - Finding time for each area: curriculum, teaching, assessment, behaviour, and safeguarding.
>
> *Great CPD. Poor CPD. What are the Signs? (Tom Sherrington, 2019)*

Talk:Write reflects the best; rejects the rest!

Reflecting the experiences of providing high quality support for heads and schools throughout the pandemic by use of technology, this programme of CPD for teachers is provided as a series of videos that may be watched as one whole day of in-service training (inset) or as a series of staff meetings – to suit the school's own agenda and to cater for the pressures of time on the school and staff diaries.

Having watched the programme, teachers are then able to refer back to video content – re-watching as much or as little as they need to refresh and support developing practice. New staff can be given access to the same quality input that existing staff had and the videos – or excerpts from them – may be used in communication with governors, parents, or other interested parties working within the school.

This publication provides a thorough analysis of the entire system, accompanied by many examples, illustrations, teaching ideas, activities, and models. It may be used to support use of the videos or as a resource in its own right and it is envisaged that all teachers would have access to this publication.

Schools may wish to nominate a Talk:Write leader to co-ordinate the programme, a leader who will work closely with the leadership team and year or phase leaders to ensure confidence, clarity, and consistency across the school. Teams should be supported to interpret and implement the programme, ensuring all reflect the school's agreed approaches. Best practice and impact will be shared and celebrated, and the whole school and its community will be fully aware of the ongoing improvements in communication skills across the school.

Talk:Write is designed to be deployed across the whole school and the whole curriculum, however it is as effective for the pupils involved if deployment is confined to one phase, one year, or even one class. Thus, a school may trial the system within a more limited forum prior to rolling it out across the school when the impact has been proven.

As with all new programmes, school leaders should plan thoroughly in advance, resource as appropriate, and support staff with persistence yet patience. The initial impact of the programme will be seen in classrooms within the first term of implementation. It will affect children's communication skills in both oracy and writing for life, providing the school is thorough and committed to the long-term change involved. However, the programme

also results in discernible and immediate impact, and thus may be relied on as a highly effective intervention.

Talk:Write will work alongside existing school programmes for talk, reading, and writing – complementing them and enhancing them. A school may, for example, retain its current phonics programme in full, whilst implementing the five 'S' system for spelling *(see Chapter 5 - The 5 'S' System for Spelling)* for complex or irregular words of high challenge. In addition, because the programme thrives best when implemented across the curriculum, this system does not take up significant time from the English curriculum or timetable. It is mainly addressed within the existing, allocated subject time of the curriculum.

What is Talk:Write?

- Talk:Write is an easily-accessed programme that raises standards in talk, communication, writing, and the general range and richness of vocabulary and language structures for pupils in English speaking schools.
- It is a system for enriching language in order to improve both the quality of talk and the quality of writing.
- It ensures that all children can talk and write confidently in Standard English.
- These actions will naturally lead to an improvement in the ability to read, to learn through reading, and to enjoy reading.
- The system consists of the teaching of sophisticated features for writing, ensuring understanding of the structure and organisation of content for writing, and building and maintaining stamina for writing.

- Within this programme, children have the opportunity to study examples of different speech codes and to enjoy exploring speech in different codes as they develop and embed their capacity to speak and write in Standard English.
- This programme includes the five 'S' system for spelling – a new and highly effective approach to teaching the spelling of irregular and challenging vocabulary.

The Importance of Talk

Talk:Write is the progression of all my previous work regarding the underpinning principles of the impact of talk on writing. The cruciality of talk as a tool in learning and communication is now, at last, nationally recognised – as is reflected in the report from Oxford University Press, *Why Closing the Word Gap Matters* (2021). The report is both thorough and interesting, however it does include the commonly held opinion that in order to learn a wider range of vocabulary most children need to read more.

In fact, many children will not learn new vocabulary through reading as their brains are not programmed to learn, understand, and retain new words at only one meeting. Most children need to meet, use, and spell new words repeatedly in order to embed them in long-term memory – and yet the reverse of the commonly held notion is true – *improving their vocabulary will improve their reading ability*. We clearly need to be teaching new words in ways different from purely reading them.

McKeown, Beck, Omanson, and Pople in *Some Effects of the Nature and Frequency of Vocabulary Instruction on the Knowledge of Use of Words* (1985), found that even a few encounters with new vocabulary were often not enough, saying that:

> ❝
>
> *...while 4 encounters with a word did not reliably improve reading comprehension, 12 encounters did.*

This opinion is now reinforced by research which strongly advocates immersion in new vocabulary, meeting and using it in as many contexts as possible, in order for it to become a part of a child's lexicon. In his article, *Reading Comprehension Requires Knowledge of Words and the World – Scientific Insights into the Fourth-Grade Slump and the Nation's Stagnant Comprehension Scores* (2008), E.D. Hirsch Jr advocates immersion in a subject or topic over a period of weeks so that new vocabulary is securely embedded. He says:

> ❝
>
> *Vocabulary researchers agree that to get a good start in learning the connotations of a word, a person needs multiple exposures to the word in different contexts. Such exposure is not supplied by a fragmented selection of reading in which topics leap from a day at the beach to a trip to the vegetable section of the supermarket.*

Hirsch goes on to say that:

> **"**
>
> *...immersion in a topic not only improves reading and develops vocabulary, it also develops writing skill.*

This would support the belief of many in education that teaching several subjects at once through a thematic approach not only strengthens the ability to make cross-curricular links, but also reinforces the pupil's understanding of the technical and process language involved, and improves the retention of new and relevant language as it is deployed across a range of contexts. In planning for short-term learning, teachers should plan to use new target language in as many contexts and across as many subjects as possible. The Talk:Write system embraces this best practice.

Hirsch proceeds to explain the cruciality of understanding the great limitations of our working memories as reported by George A. Miller in *The Psychology of Communication* (1968); including the knowledge that working memory can only retain seven facts – plus or minus two – at any one time. This limitation appears to be regardless of ability or intelligence, although by the gathering of a number of facts under one heading or label, larger volumes of information may be recalled. It is because of this restriction of retention in working memory that Hirsch argues that the faster we are able to decode text, the quicker we are able to deploy it to long-term memory and move forward:

> **"**
>
> *One way we overcome this limitation of working memory while reading is by learning how to make a rapid, automatic deployment of underlying reading processes so that they become fast and unconscious, leaving the conscious mind (i.e. the working memory) free to think about what a text means. This is why fast and accurate decoding is important.*

Thus, two children reading the same text for the same length of time will retain quite different amounts of knowledge or information, including the retention of new words learnt through the process of decoding, purely because one reader knows considerably more of the words in the text prior to accessing it and therefore has to spend significantly less time in decoding unknown words.

Hirsch says:

> **"**
>
> *...word-rich children learn more vocabulary and content than word-poor children from the very same language experiences.*

It is now widely accepted in research that adequate reading comprehension depends on a person already knowing between 90 and 95 percent of the words in a text. Hirsch likens this to the way the young child acquires early vocabulary and language:

> Knowing that percentage of words allows the reader to get the main thrust of what is being said and therefore to guess correctly what the unfamiliar words probably mean. (This inferential process is, of course, how we pick up oral language in early childhood and it sustains our vocabulary growth throughout our lives.)

Dale and O'Rourke in *Vocabulary Building* (1986) talk about four 'levels' of word knowledge:

> 1. *I never saw it before.*
> 2. *I've heard of it, but I don't know what it means.*
> 3. *I recognize it in context – it has something to do with…*
> 4. *I know it.*

Many pupils show a lack of appropriate and enriched vocabulary that has primarily arisen from spending so little time engaged in positive and extended conversation, discussion, or debate with family members at home. This situation is now also exacerbated for children from quite a young age, by their spending so long on technology.

It is incumbent upon schools and teachers to ensure that all children know and can use a wide range of vocabulary if they are to make best progress. When considering ability to decode texts and extrapolate information, however, it is also important to consider the child's ability to concentrate for extended periods of time. In *What are Normal Attention Spans for Children?* (Christina M. Ward, 2020), attention spans are summarised as being two to three minutes for every year that a child has been alive. Thus, a five-year-old may concentrate for ten minutes while a nine-year-old may achieve 18 to 20 minutes of concentration.

The teaching of vocabulary outside of reading improves reading. Doctor Todd Risley (1937 – 2007) states, in *Meaningful Differences in the Everyday Lives of Young American Children* (1995), that widening children's vocabulary will improve their reading.

> If you already had the oral vocabulary, you knew the words you were reading, you experienced them as part of your oral vocabulary, then reading was easy.

A child can decode words better in advanced text if they already have the words in their lexicon – that is, they already know and understand them. Thus, improving vocabulary improves the decoding of text. That is not to say that reading with children is not crucially important in the Early Years and throughout primary education. It instils a love of story, of language, and of the rhythms and patterns of language. It is intimate and reassuring and enriching, and – as a child becomes more competent and more able to retain new words at fewer exposures – it can introduce new vocabulary.

Risley goes on to say that a failure to address this disadvantage for word-poor children leads to the gap between the word-rich and the word-poor growing wider as they move through school.

> **"**
>
> *In vocabulary acquisition, a small early advantage grows into a much bigger one unless we intervene very intelligently to help the disadvantaged student learn words at an accelerated rate.*

The number of words known by an individual varies greatly according to the sources of the statistics. The average adult may be quoted as knowing between 20 and 30,000 words, yet other sources say up to 50,000. Equally, the statistics given for children are insecure, but a useful estimate is around the number equivalent to their age in thousands. Thus, a seven-year-old may know around 7,000 words and a ten-year-old around 10,000.

However, Risley stated that the average adult in the world of work knew, by definition and usage, between 20,000 and 30,000 words, whereas the average adult on state benefit knew only around 12,000. This could be an implied impact of the outcome of being word-rich or word-poor.

The Changes Involved in Becoming a Writer

Writing is a complex process that requires pupils to be equally proficient in four different sets of skills, all at the same time, to be fully effective. These are:

1. **The quality of language written:** The range of appropriate, interesting and – sometimes – sophisticated vocabulary, written in engaging sentences with correct grammatical structures.

2. **The basic skills of producing writing on paper:** Grammar, spelling, handwriting, and accurate use of punctuation.

3. **The correct response to a stimulus:** This includes appropriate content and reflects features of the genre or type of text the stimulus requires: poetry, recount, report, instruction, explanation, persuasion, discussion, dialogue, questionnaire, or the full range of fiction genres e.g. historical, scientific, mystery, adventure, etc.

4. **Writing stamina:** This enables the child to sustain the process of writing for an extended period without deterioration of the quality or content.

To be a fully effective writer, accurate use of grammar, handwriting, spelling, and punctuation should be programmed into a pupil's sub-conscious so that the working brain can focus completely on *what* is being written rather than *how* it is being written. Programming requires frequent teaching and practise until the writer produces almost totally accurate writing every time they write and can find almost all basic errors without support, on a re-read.

Besides being 'programmed' to operate the first two skill sets without conscious thought the majority of the time (the ability to work with automaticity), children must also develop the stamina to complete a sustained piece of writing to age-appropriate length at one sitting, followed by proof reading and – following feedback or marking – editing and improving.

Talk:Write addresses the first and fourth skill sets, the quality and accuracy of language, both spoken and written, and the stamina to sustain the quality of a piece of extended writing at one sitting. It also supports the accuracy of deployment of basic skills.

The Impact of Talk on Writing

Talk:Write also addresses the issue of local talk, colloquial talk, local accents, and dialects – and provides solutions to the need for accurate grammar and spelling (Standard English). Talk:Write also integrates the important element of stamina with style into its systems. Finally, it gives steps for teaching the fundamental skills of writing: handwriting, spelling, and use of a range of punctuation, without which we cannot write coherently. It does not provide schemes of work for teaching these skills however, which remain the province of the school.

Local dialects are a valued part of our history and celebrate the cultural differences of our communities – and thus they should be preserved. However, there are many children in inner cities and in isolated communities whose speech consists entirely of a strong local accent and / or a dialect. If that is the only version of English they possess, then that is the version they will speak or write in, however important the task. Talk:Write explores dialects and promotes activities to enable children to switch easily and consciously between alternative versions of English and Standard English (code switching) and to respect the speech of other cultures and communities in the United Kingdom and around the world.

To write correctly, children need to be able to talk confidently and fluently in Standard English. However, it is important to note that Standard English is not 'better' than other forms of English discussed in this publication, but rather happens to be the agreed form for national and international communication.

This Publication Provides

1. An analysis of the process of Talk:Write for improving the quality of speech and writing in schools.
2. From dialect to suave speak. Using dialects from around the United Kingdom and the wider world, with suggestions for activities to clarify variations in spoken language, Standard English, and suave speak.
3. An analysis of the main features of spoken and written language, known as suave features.
4. Exemplification of introductory activities for different age groups.
5. Ideas for teaching activities and games (embedding activities for development of writer's voice in classrooms).
6. Guidance and support for teaching children new to English.

All these are implemented in enjoyable ways that maintain total respect for different communities and localities and recognise that – for many – speaking in the codes of their communities is essential for their integration.

This approach is rooted in a firm belief in the importance of talk.

In summary, our mantra is:

> If a child can't say it,
> a child can't write it!

This mantra has now been further developed to:

> If a child can't say it in Standard English, a child can't write it in Standard English!

Chapter 1 – Why Talk Is an Issue

The teaching profession has become increasingly aware of the impact of language deprivation on standards in education over past decades. Many young children are entering school around the age of four with very limited vocabulary and an inability to express themselves with confidence and fluency. This causes serious delays in learning across the majority of the curriculum, and yet the cause of the learning delay is directly attributable to the child's home life and not to the world of education. There are two main causes of this worrying factor.

The Impact of the Word Gap

In 2003, Hart and Risley published *The Early Catastrophe: The 30 Million Word Gap by Age 3* which caused a storm of incredulity – both that the evidence was there and that no-one had known it. Their findings were challenged in a 2018 article *Re-examining the Verbal Environments of Children From Different Socio-economic Backgrounds* written by Douglas Sperry (Lead Researcher at St Mary of the Woods College, Indiana) and colleagues, who cited their own research, which failed to find a correlation between socio-economic status and the number of words a child heard. However, their findings were devalued when

it was shown that they failed to replicate the full circumstances of Risley and Hart's work. Their paper also sparked a debate on whether words heard in the conversations of others had similar impact to words spoken directly to the child.

Since the publication of Risley and Hart's findings, other research has shown that the word gap may – in fact – be more like four million words heard (not all different words – many may be repeated words) at age four rather than 30 million. However, the consensus is that there *is* a word gap, that it is significant, and that it impacts dramatically on a child's learning and development.

In his interview with David Boulton (*Children of the Code*, 2009), Risley qualified his findings by saying that the underpinning issue was whether parents could be classified as 'talkative' or 'taciturn'. Risley and Hart's study had shown that all parents, regardless of socio-economic classification or personal level of 'talkativeness', did business talk with their children. Business talk is the instruction, questioning, or comment necessary to enable a child to function throughout the day. It is usually characterised by short, simple sentences without embellishment or extension.

Examples of business talk in a home are: *'Eat your food.'*; *'Don't interrupt.'*; *'Do your homework.'*; *'Where's your coat?'*; *'Go to bed!'*

Talkative parents, however, extended their talk greatly through responding to the child's answers, asking additional questions, providing explanations, description or detail, and offering further commentary. Taciturn parents rarely developed their conversations in this way.

Risley stated that talkative parents raise talkative children and that taciturn parents raise taciturn children.

> We need to educate the parent bodies of our schools on the importance of talking at length with their children.

Government sources have reported on the impact of lockdown during the world pandemic on the speech of young children. This is not a phenomenon of lockdown; it is purely an extension of the impact of a home with taciturn parents. The nursery and Early Years' experience for young children in a school is crucial in beginning the journey of compensating for language deprivation caused in the home.

The Importance of Conversation

The subject matter of the conversation is not important. Local accent or dialect is not a detriment. It is the process of talk, the patterning of language, and the amount of exposure to vocabulary and phraseology that is crucial. Both Risley and Gabrieli pointed out that the child from an impoverished home

could articulate as confidently as one from a privileged home, albeit in a local form of speech, providing at least one of the parents is a talker.

John Gabrieli, professor of brain and cognitive sciences and a member of MIT's McGovern Institute for Brain Research, published a paper – *Psychological Studies* (April 2018) – on the power of conversation in the brain development of children:

The really novel thing about our paper is that it provides the first evidence that family conversation at home is associated with brain development in children. It's almost magical how parental conversation appears to influence the biological growth of the brain.

While researchers know that the word gap exists, there was little to no information on the underlying mechanism of what the gap means regarding brain differences and cognitive skills. By recruiting subjects at different income levels, and collecting brain image studies, the researchers hoped to learn exactly what the gap means for children as they grow up.

Ann Trafton comments in *The Power of Talking with Children* (April 2018):

> "
>
> *MIT cognitive scientists have now found that back-and-forth conversation between a child and an adult is more critical to language development than the word gap. In a study of kids aged four to six, differences in the number of 'conversational turns' accounted for a large portion of the differences in brain physiology and language skills, regardless of parental income or education.*

The recordings made during the research described above were analysed and the number of words spoken by the child, the number of words spoken by an adult to the child, and how many conversational turns the children and adults took were all calculated. There was a strong correlation between higher scores on all tests (including grammar, vocabulary, and verbal reasoning) and the number of conversations the children had engaged in. Gabrieli says there was also a close relationship between these conversations and how active the Broca's area of the brain was while the children listened to stories in the MRI scanner. Broca's area is a region of the brain linked to speech production. It is located in the frontal lobe of the dominant hemisphere usually to the left of the brain.

The number of words heard and spoken by children was not as closely associated with brain activity and performance on tests, thus the actual conversations were the key, not income, education, or number of words.

While it is a fact that children in higher income homes are generally exposed to more language, the data from the study showed that children from lower income homes could have test scores (the usual measure of performance and progress in the United States of America) and Broca activity similar to their wealthier playmates, if they had considerable amounts of conversation happening on a daily basis. Whether the words spoken were influenced by local accent, or even included vocabulary only found in a particular dialect, is also irrelevant to this study. The impact on brain development would be similar.

Gabrieli summarised the work, writing:

> "
>
> *In our analysis, the conversational turn-taking seems like the thing that makes a difference, regardless of socio-economic status. Such turn-taking occurs more often in families from a higher socio-economic status, but children coming from families with lesser income or parental education showed the same benefits from conversational turn-taking.*

This has an important consequence for schools and teachers, as the groundwork is done – or not done – before the child enters school. As Gabrieli said, the greatest impact comes from being *directly addressed* by the individual, not just through passive presence in the conversations of others. This is a crucial aspect of understanding differences in performance as speakers and in seeking to remediate for this in Early Years settings. The degree to which the dominant parent or carer in the young child's life directly engages that child in extended talk, even before the child can speak themselves, is usually the main determiner in how articulate that child will become.

A further factor in some children's inability to develop rich, extended conversation today is technology. From a very young age, many children grow up in front of screens of varying sizes and purposes. These electronic devices are extremely efficient at keeping young children engaged and entertained, and thus the child does not demand the attention of adults as often or for as long as the child without technology. It is not unusual for some children to spend almost all their waking non-school time in front of either a TV or social media or an electronic game of some sort. Even meals are frequently taken on knees in front of 'the tech'. Interacting with technology does expose children to talk, however the question is – does it enhance a child's verbal skills? The research emphasises the importance of the exposure to speech being through direct contact, usually with interaction, and not through passive reception through technology such as TV or electronic games.

Does the Code of Talk Matter?

This has huge implications for how and what we teach in primary schools. Simply aiming to teach children to 'talk better' is not enough. We need to enable all children, not just those of the talkative parents, to talk fluently, with confidence, and at length, using a wide range of vocabulary and language features that make the structure and content interesting for the listener. The research quoted here clearly shows that, while this is not just a socio-economic syndrome – although there are generally more children from poorer

homes suffering from speech deprivation than from wealthier homes – technology is impacting on children from all homes. In addition, many parents from affluent homes today are working long hours and may be suffering great stresses and pressures from the impact of the times on their professional lives. They may find making quality time for their children difficult and stress can also lead to communication becoming limited in any home. Many parents raising a family in poverty will also be highly stressed, and possibly anxious, and both these scenarios can lead to even the most talkative of adults reducing their interaction to pure business talk.

Many children live in localities that have distinctive spoken accents and / or dialects. Children raised in homes where all they hear is people talking with a pronounced local accent or dialect will speak in the same way. This may be the only form of English many children know. It is crucial that these children learn to speak in Standard English in school, as they will need to both speak and write in Standard English confidently in order to communicate their ideas and their learning effectively and to be more socially and academically successful as they grow and mature. Yet, at the same time, it is crucial that their self-esteem and the esteem of the family and the community are not damaged by apparent criticism or belittlement of the way they speak. Accents and dialects are part of the heritage of many countries and as such must be valued and cherished. Street talk and patois are both forms of local dialect and should not be derided by any sector of the country.

Local accent – whether urban or rural – is about identity, culture, and belonging, but children need to be bilingual and able to switch easily between the speech of their locality and Standard English for presentation and writing, if they usually speak in any code other than Standard English. In addition, many pupils are already learning to communicate in English as a second, third, or even fourth language. They have to switch easily and swiftly between home languages and English, before starting the process of converting the local accent they have developed into Standard English for use in a specific context, and then switching back to their usual speech and thinking languages for integration into their communities.

> This ease of switching between different forms of talk is called **code switching**.

Enabling children to become confident and fluent speakers in Standard English as well as in their community codes must be one of the top priorities for children aged 4 to 12. The earlier the intervention and the more prolonged and consistent it is throughout the years of primary education, the better the outcomes will be. It must be emphasised that speaking in Standard English does not mean with no local accent, but rather with the accepted grammatical codes and structures for language. Many of us speak in grammatically correct English while still retaining the accent of the locality we grew up in.

This is *not* just a matter of teaching children to 'talk posh' through elocution-type lessons. Children need more talk in their lives; the code of talk is not the only priority in developing the linguistic capacity of a child's brain.

A programme is needed that promotes quality talk within and between lessons, whether it is discussing or debating issues and events within a subject, planning and devising ways forward in work, or explaining and justifying ideas, conclusions, or thoughts, or when waiting to move to another lesson,

to lunch, to breaks, or to assembly. These 'waiting' times can be better utilised with quick games and activities to embed language features or for pupils to do a two-minute presentation on how their learning, understanding, or thinking has progressed in the previous lesson.

Ideally, such a programme would also be as effective and efficient whether it is implemented as a whole-school programme, across one year or one phase of education only, or purely by one class teacher who seeks to see an improvement in standards of speech and writing in a class. It should be able to be supported, strengthened, and enhanced by classroom support staff, and even taught by staff other than qualified teachers when identified by leadership. It might also be implemented short-term in classrooms as an intervention, although the principles of high expectations for quality of speech and writing must then be maintained and short boosters or refreshers be deployed as needed.

Such a vital programme should be fully understood and advocated by all involved in the school – by support staff, parents, governors, supervisors, and all others who make contact with the pupil body. For some within these groups, there may be implications for induction into the different codes of speech and for what Standard English does constitute and does not constitute.

> The more all adults are able to interact with pupils, enjoying the discussions on what has been said or heard, and initiating conversations in any setting or situation, the more the culture of valuing talk and language will pervade the school.

And Why Fun?

Above all, the programme should be both rigorous and enjoyable. It is vital to remember that children who are enjoying the learning will be actively engaged within discussions and activities, they absorb the learning more easily and will retain it better over time.

> "
>
> *The truth is that when we scrub joy and comfort from the classroom, we distance our students from effective information processing and long-term memory storage. Instead of taking pleasure from learning, students become bored, anxious, and anything but engaged. They ultimately learn to feel bad about school and lose the joy they once felt.*
>
> **The Neuroscience of Joyful Education (Jenny Willis, 2007)**

> "
>
> *Results of the experiment show that, thanks to joyful lectures, students are not only happier, but they also remember more information, even if topics relate to purely business problems. Despite the fact that in the case of accounting, the results of the experiment are not so clear, in the case of management classes students evaluated funny classes as better than traditional ones. They also remembered more information. That's why we can put forward a thesis that one of the barriers to learning is a rigid and serious way of teaching.*
>
> **The Effect of Enjoyment on Learning (J. Hernik, E. Jaworska, 2018)**

A programme that provides all this for a school would be an essential and urgent priority.

> That programme is Talk:Write!

Chapter 2 – Launching Talk:Write

Talk:Write is easy to incorporate into a school's existing curriculum and timetable. Its effectiveness is increased through exposure across the existing curriculum, bearing in mind the need for up to 12 experiences with new language in a range of learning across a similar theme in order for all children to embed the new vocabulary and structures. Teaching through a thematic approach to the curriculum complements the work needed to embed new speech codes and new features of language through relevant games and activities. It enables re-enforcement through multiple uses in a wide range of contexts.

This programme is also highly flexible. A school may adopt all of it and apply it across the whole school, or may focus on particular aspects where their most urgent need lies. One phase or year of a school may implement the programme while others do not, or one class – alone – may implement it.

Implementing Talk:Write

In Talk:Write, the word suave is used to mean ambitious or sophisticated.

1. Make all learning and activities fun, encouraging appropriate laughter, but with constant respect for the speech and codes of speech of others.

2. Explain the differences between the five codes of speech: local speak, dialect, Standard English, suave speak, and writer's voice in both spoken and written language, with examples. Focus on these in the five short sessions and within lessons across the curriculum for one or two weeks (see Chapter 3 – The 5 Codes of Speech).

3. Explore the structure and use of dialects (see Chapter 3 – The 5 Codes of Speech). This may all be done within one week for older children but may be over two or more weeks with younger children.

4. Conduct parts of lessons or whole sessions in different codes e.g. in adapted dialects or in suave speak for enjoyment. There is no expectation that children should learn a dialect unless they wish to – only that they should have experience of them.

5. Use popular nursery rhymes and excerpts from stories, historic movies, etc. to illustrate writer's voice. There is a wide range of contemporary, diverse, or classical children's literature that should be shared with children, such as 'Wind in the Willows', 'The Jungle Book', and 'Peter Pan'.

6. Use video clips, recordings, and short scripts to illustrate dialects and local accents.

7. Teach the five suave features of language through an ongoing programme of short, fun sessions. These, applied through Standard English, will form the child's personal writer's voice *(see Chapter 4 - The 5 Suave Features of Language)*.

8. Teach children to speak in Standard English and suave speak whilst still valuing their own local speak, whether that be accent or dialect. Pupils who speak only in Standard English will enjoy exposure to other forms of speech and may have fun making up their own short presentations in their own interpretations of a dialect. Move easily between different forms of speech in role play and discussions.

9. Play fun games and complete activities throughout the ongoing programme of short, fun sessions to embed new vocabulary and structures *(see Chapter 10 - Games, Activities, and Examples)*.

10. Build stamina for extended writing *(see Chapter 7 - Stamina with Style)*.

11. Teach the five 'S' system for spelling *(see Chapter 5 - The 5 'S' System for Spelling)*.

12. Establish and maintain the weekly suave writing session *(see Chapter 6 - The Suave Writing Session)*.

A glossary of Talk:Write terminology is provided, *see page 129.*

Time Allocation for Talk:Write

1. The Five Weekly Short Sessions

Four of the five weekly short sessions last between 10 and 15 minutes and are spread throughout the week. There may be more than one session planned into the same day. These sessions are to explore speech codes, talk in different codes, play games to embed suave words and other new features of language, and take part in other fun activities.

The decision for when these should take place each week might be managed by the school, left to the team leader, or remain the responsibility of the class teacher.

Class teachers could slot the sessions in at different times each week to work around the time needed for the different subjects on the timetable. One or more of the sessions might actually be part of the warm-up or cool-down of a lesson or be slotted into the middle as a break.

Year team leaders or phase leaders might pre-timetable all the sessions for classes in their teams, or pre-timetable two or three and leave the others for the class teacher to embed in other learning. Timetabled sessions may be before or after a break, an assembly or lunch, or within a subject other than English.

The strength of pre-timetabled sessions is that they enable re-assurance that the process is taking place through walk-about. They also facilitate support for teachers new to the system, peer observations for coaching, and sharing best practice.

2. The Planning Short Session

One of the short sessions should be used in the last 15 minutes of the lesson that occurs immediately before the extended and unsupported writing session. It includes five minutes for games and activities to refresh the latest suave word, and ten minutes planning and preparation time.

3. The Suave Writing Session

Each week, there is one extended and unsupported writing session (the suave writing session) of between 10 to 30 minutes for children aged 5 to 7, and up to 50 minutes for children aged 8 to 12. There should be an additional 5 to 10 minutes soon after this session for the child to re-read their own writing and correct any mistakes they find, using insertion marks to add suave words before the teacher or anyone else reads the piece, gives feedback, or makes suggestions.

The extended writing session should be planned into the curriculum for the same time every week and thus is the responsibility of year leaders, phase leaders, or senior managers.

It should always be towards the end of the week on either a Thursday or a Friday, and ideally should be immediately after the mid-morning break. Children will come in from the playground calmly and quietly, managed by members of staff, and should go to their tables in silence to commence their writing. The preparation will have been in the short session immediately before play.

All classes will therefore be writing in silence at the same time, ensuring that a quiet and calm atmosphere pervades the corridor or school.

Exemplar Suave Writing Session Timetable

1. 5 minutes refreshment activities using words and phrases introduced recently.
2. 10 minutes planning in the manner of their choice.
3. Playtime.
4. Suave writing session of age-appropriate duration (up to 50 minutes for ages 8 to 12).
5. Read through.
6. Return to normal curriculum.

4. Suave Writing Homework

There is one whole-class suave writing homework the night before the extended writing session to prepare ideas for the writing through discussion with family members. A relevant suave word might be provided for inclusion in the discussions. This may be a suave word the class have already met or it may be a new word. If it is new, the class should have had the time to embed it, for example through the five 'S' system for spelling.

The purpose of the homework the night before the suave writing session should be explained as an opportunity for the family to help the child clarify their ideas and collect further suggestions on the planned topic for writing. Parents should be told that no notes or pre-prepared writing need to be done and should not be done. The function is to discuss ideas and may also be used to help embed a new word. They should be asked to turn technology off and sit together, possibly sharing a meal, as they discuss the topic for this week. If a target suave word has also been given in the homework instruction, parents are asked to use the target word as often as possible.

The subject for the class homework will be whatever the children are to write about the next day. Thus, it may be an imaginary story or may be related to learning taking place in one of the subjects of the week e.g. the diary of a Roman soldier, a Viking, an astronaut, or a cast-away on a desert island; a letter home from a soldier in the trenches in World War One, or from an explorer in the Amazon jungle; a persuasive piece to the Tudors to clean up their streets and towns, or to world leaders from Greta Thunberg; etc.

There is no fixed time allocation for the homework. The aim is that the discussions feel organic and enjoyable, and that they positively affect attitudes to talk at home. A usual homework task might be 30 to 45 minutes long, so use this as a guide.

Children might take home a message that says:

Suave Writing Homework

Homework tonight is to talk about the explorer who discovered the Amazon Rainforest for Europeans in 1541. Can we talk about things we might have seen in the rainforest, if we had been with him? Who were the people already living in the rainforest? What adventures might we have had? What would we see and hear? We have pictures from rainforests on our website to help us.

We have a new suave word to use in this work. It is 'humid' and it means very hot and damp weather that makes us sweat. Please can we all try to use 'humid' in a sentence about being in a rainforest?

5. Suave Word Homework

There is one whole-school suave word homework at the start of each week launched through assembly, giving the same new suave word to all children in the school and a context in which to use it in talk with all the family that night. These words should be ambitious, but quite short (words of one or two syllables) to enable children of all ages to achieve success in spelling. Examples could be words such as suave, perky, angst, conceal, and devour. A range are available *(see Chapter 10 - Games, Activities, and Examples)* and on our website.

The teacher could fit a five 'S' system for spelling session into the day, before the children take the word home, to ensure that they can remember how to pronounce it and what it means.

It is important for the whole school to have the same word to make the evening's conversation manageable and of high quality for families. In this case, teachers of older children (aged 8 to 12) should give children additional, complex words to learn and use later in the week.

If this is not considered to be an option by the management of the school, it is suggested that two different words might be given weekly, on two different days. The younger children (aged 5 to 7) might receive their word on Mondays and the older children (aged 8 to 12) might receive theirs on Tuesdays.

Families will need to be inducted into suave word homework through a positive introduction on the importance of talk in learning new vocabulary and in preparing ideas for writing.

Explain to parents that the purpose of the suave word homework is to introduce a new suave word of the week for the whole school. Families are asked to talk about the word, spell the word, and play games or make up sentences with the word in it.

A context for the homework chat might be suggested to help families to use the word appropriately, if they are struggling to find ideas for themselves. The subject for chat might be something happening in the local news, the country's news or world news, something important happening in the local area or in the school, or something similar. If it is something some parents may find it hard to think of ideas for, a few examples might be given. For example topics, *(see Chapter 10 – Games, Activities, and Examples).*

There is no fixed time allocation for the homework. The main purpose is to give pupils opportunities to practise using new suave words. This task should last up to 30 minutes. At the end of the afternoon of a day with suave word homework, a message is sent to all homes that says something like:

Suave Word Homework

Our suave word of the week is 'crave'.

Please can we turn the TV and gaming technology off for this homework? Crave means to want something very badly. Everyone could talk about one thing they would crave to eat for supper, or one present they would crave to receive for their birthday. They could talk about people they would crave to meet or places they might crave to visit. Please help your child to practise this word and to use it in their talk. Thank you.

Exemplar Weekly Timetable

Monday	Tuesday	Wednesday	Thursday	Friday
Maths	Maths	Talk:Write 2	Maths	English
English	Music	English	Talk:Write 4: Planning	Science
Playtime	Playtime	Playtime	Assembly	Playtime
Assembly	Assembly	Assembly	Playtime	Assembly
Geography	English	Maths	Suave Writing Session	Maths
Science	Science	Talk:Write 3	Music	Maths
Lunch	Lunch	Lunch	Lunch	Lunch
History	Talk:Write 1	D and T	PE	Talk:Write 5
PE	Art	RE	History	Geography
Suave Word Homework 1	Suave Word Homework 2*	Suave Writing Homework	Maths Homework	Reading Homework

* Only required if doing two sets as described on the previous page.
For weekly plan examples, *(see Chapter 10 – Games, Activities, and Examples).*

Chapter 3 – The 5 Codes of Speech

There are five codes of spoken English that children may meet in their daily lives:

- Local accents.
- Dialects (including street talk and patois).
- Standard English.
- Sophisticated speech or received pronunciation, known as suave speak in Talk:Write.
- Writer's voice.

Within a community, there may be families who speak entirely in any one of these codes and other families who speak in a mix of these codes, changing their speech for purpose. All children, however, need to learn to speak and write confidently in Standard English, as this is the accepted code for national and international communication. The aim of this section is to introduce and explain the process of children understanding and respecting the different codes found in the communities where they live, and to support them in developing their own codes for different purposes.

It is important that children are not made to feel ashamed of the way they speak. It is also important that they are not made to feel they should no longer speak in their local accent or dialect, as retaining it is a crucial element of continuing to feel accepted in their community.

The 5 Codes of Speech

1. **Local Speak:** Many children will have grown up in localities that have a strong local accent that alters the pronunciation (and – if left unaddressed – the spelling) of words and phrases in Standard English. These children need to learn to switch between their local accent and suave speak, as appropriate for setting and purpose. Some local accents include a small number of dialect words – especially from patois or street talk – and may have noun/verb mismatches, although the language is not a dialect per se. It is vital that all references to local accent and to dialects are made with the greatest of respect. Children who do not have a local accent may enjoy using one in role play or videos – again, while showing respect. Being able to retain and value their heritage speech is, for many children, essential if the child wishes to continue to blend into their home community.

2. **Dialect:** Some children will have grown up in localities where almost all people speak in a local dialect, street talk, or patois. These change the grammatical structures of Standard English into a local structure and also

include dialect-specific vocabulary that does not exist in Standard English. These children need to learn to modify their speech into local speak when appropriate, and into Standard English when appropriate. Children who have never spoken in dialect will enjoy quoting some of the examples given in this publication, making up scripts with dialect in, and using rich forms of dialect in speech and role play. Classes may enjoy making up their own class dialect using some of the words they like from their lessons and even making up their own new words. Being able to retain and value their heritage speech is, however, essential if the child wishes to continue to blend into their community.

3. **Standard English:** Some children will already talk in Standard English. Indeed, some schools will be based in areas where the entire population speaks in Standard English. For these children, an understanding of the variations of English spoken in the United Kingdom and in the wider world will support future interaction and communication, tolerance, and pride in being part of a language that has become the most widely used in the world. These children will still need to learn to include a range of suave features in their daily talk as appropriate, in order to become suave writers.

4. **Suave Speak:** The inclusion of sophisticated language (called suave features in Talk:Write) into speech executed in Standard English. When transferred into writing, this becomes the writer's voice. Children may enjoy using suave speak with a more refined accent, as in received pronunciation.

5. **Writer's Voice:** The personal style of an accomplished writer, often associated with historical and traditional writing forms.

Introducing Dialects and Effective Code Switching

1. Explain the differences between local speak, dialect, Standard English, suave speak, and writer's voice in both spoken and written language, with examples. Explore the structure and use of dialects.

2. Conduct parts of lessons or whole sessions in different codes e.g. in dialect or in suave speak. Ensure this is done in a light-hearted and fun way.

3. Use popular nursery rhymes and excerpts from stories, historic movies, etc. to illustrate writer's voice.

4. Use video clips, recordings, and short scripts *(see Chapter 10 - Games, Activities, and Examples)* to illustrate dialects and local speak in use.

5. Make up your own class dialect, using dialect words the children like and some made up words for purpose. Have fun conversing in the class dialect, but always emphasise respect for the way different people and communities speak.

6. Teach children to speak in Standard English and suave speak, and to experiment with local speak if that is not the code they usually use, switching easily between the three on command (code switching), using discussions, short scripts, and role play with individuals allocated a type of code they are to use.

7. Teach the suave features of language through English lessons and an ongoing programme of short, fun sessions in order to develop their own writer's voice *(see Chapter 4 - The 5 Suave Features of Language)*.

8. Play fun games and complete activities through the ongoing programme of short, fun sessions to embed new vocabulary and other suave features *(see Chapter 10 – Games, Activities, and Examples)*.

The process of teaching and developing language through Talk:Write is intended to be both little and often, and easy and enjoyable. It should permeate the school week every week throughout each academic year, becoming as natural to the children as reading, writing, researching, talking in general, and thinking.

The five short sessions a week to consolidate and develop language skills are an essential part of the Talk:Write process. However, it is the additional opportunities for practising and embedding new techniques, strategies, and vocabulary across the wider curriculum in taught slots, in talking slots within existing lessons, and in the 'waiting' times between lessons, before assembly, playtime, lunchtime, or home time that is the strength of the system. For example, if a class are in the process of learning two new words (e.g. the verb 'detect' and the adjective 'disastrous'), pupils might be asked to work one or both into their talk about global warming, volcanic eruptions, meteors, World War One, the Viking invasion of Britain, the life-cycle of the frog, friction, a poem about their school, a diary item or a group evaluation of work on balance, frozen frames, and so on, maximising the many opportunities that occur in subjects across the curriculum, and to play quick games and activities using the words while waiting to move to the next stage of the day. This is in addition to using them in the planned Talk:Write sessions.

An exemplar framework for this weekly practice is modelled later *(see Chapter 10 – Games, Activities, and Examples)*.

Whenever children talk within lessons, they should be encouraged – from a young age – to speak in Standard English, using extended sentences when they are able to, unless it is a lesson where the code of speech has been changed, for example everyone is speaking in local speak for 20 minutes. Children aged 7 to 12 should be able to move between their different codes of speech with confidence almost all the time, if they have been exposed to the process from age four or five, without being prompted by adults. Whenever children are heard to use new vocabulary or language features, they should be praised and the attention of the class should be brought to their achievement in order to promote and encourage the spread of best practice.

Talking with and to Young Children

Fill young children's lives with talk from the moment they enter the school. Ensure that children's days are filled with a wide range of rich and varied experiences and activities and that they understand all they see and do through talk, discussion, and description. This good practice has always been a priority in the majority of Early Years settings and most adults working with young children do so with great skill, developing and improving pupils' speech and vocabulary with considerable impact.

Young children should be making choices and exploring experiences freely, mixing with other children, and talking without restraint as they do. Some children may need to be encouraged to explore new experiences. Some children may need to be encouraged to mingle and talk with other children. Most children in many settings will need encouragement and support to extend their range of vocabulary and skills of oral communication. Describing things to young children and teaching them to describe things is very important.

Activities available should always include mark making of some type, including working in wet sand, paint, and modelling media. Children aged four and above should use a range of media including plastic, felt or wooden letters, wax crayons, pencil crayons, felt tips, and pencils for mark making. They should copy, trace, and use dot-to-dot models.

As they become ready, children should handle and sequence letters of the alphabet, naming them, and saying their sounds. They should learn to trace and copy their own first names and should recognise their names on coat pegs, shelves, and other equipment. They should start to label things around the classroom, with one or two-word titles.

This work will go on in parallel with the school's existing programme for teaching phonics. The teaching of phonics is a key part of the teaching of reading. The teaching of both the names and sounds of the individual letters of the alphabet is for the teaching of decoding the spelling of complex words and words that do not follow the rules of phonics in reading and for spelling them correctly in writing.

The aim for children aged three to five should be to enable them all to become confident and clear speakers able to:

- Speak aloud in a small group or with the class.
- Speak clearly without self-consciousness about speech codes.
- Use three or more short sentences at a time to say what they saw or did.

They should:

- Learn new words related to things they do and see.
- Start to describe things they do or see in their speech.
- Start to explain how they did things or how things work.
- Start to express preferences, likes, and dislikes about things they do and see.
- Learn how to describe things, giving increasing detail.

Starting the Process with Young Children

Ideally, a focus on the development of talk should commence as soon as a child enters their first Early Years or educational setting, which may be aged three or four. It should be expected that all adults will interact with young children, talking with them, asking questions, answering questions, and giving explanations as children explore their surroundings and play. The following summarises the role of the adult in nurturing and further developing the speech of young children.

The adult should:

1. Start the process from age three to five or as soon as you start to teach a class that has not met Talk:Write before.
2. Encourage talk at all times in all areas of the curriculum.
3. Encourage all pupils to listen to others with attention and show increasing respect for all other speakers when in group talks.
4. Praise children who increase their contributions.

5. Praise children who mention something or refer back to something someone else said.

6. Always repeat or summarise what a child says after the child has finished talking, slightly re-phrasing, and correcting any grammar errors if there were any. Do not comment on the grammar errors.

7. When children are comfortable talking for short periods of time, usually making two or more points, start to talk more generally about talk and the ways different people talk. Why might this be?

8. Explain the importance of showing complete respect to each other and to the ways we all speak.

9. Ask children how some of them speak differently to each other.

10. Start to introduce the five codes of speech.

1. Local Speak

1. When the children seem ready, in that they are usually talking clearly and with some confidence while extending some sentences:

   - Identify the local accent or dialect with the children. Celebrate the speaking of it.

   - Talk about the values of identity and culture in simple ways. For example, *'We like to hear people talking in different ways, don't we?'*

   - If the school serves a community where all speak in Standard English, discuss (with respect) the accents (and dialects if appropriate) heard in nearby towns and cities or spoken by people who come to work in the area. Do any members of staff have a different accent? Can any of them speak in a dialect for demonstration purposes?

2. If children in the school are not familiar with a form of local speak, introduce them to the concept. Talk about television programmes or people they have met who talked differently to them, e.g. in the market. Watch a television clip of an old series in local speak e.g. *East Enders* or *Only Fools and Horses*.

3. Identify the differences in language in a favourite book or nursery rhyme. How might character X have said that in local speak?

4. All speak in local speak for short periods during lessons or between lessons, whether they do naturally or not. Remember – local speak is just an accent, although many children may naturally use occasional words from one of the forms of dialect they hear regularly. Local speak is still a form of Standard English although there may be changes, such as in pronunciation and letters missing, from forms expected in Standard English. For some, there are small changes in grammatical structures in local speak, taken from the local dialect.

5. All show full respect for local speak and those who use it naturally every day.

6. Remember, Standard English is not the 'best' English, it is purely the agreed form for national and international communication.

Sample texts written in local speak for use with young children are available *(see Chapter 10 - Games, Activities, and Examples)* and our website.

When people make what we call 'mistakes' in their grammar when speaking or writing, it is not actually a 'mistake'. 'Mistake' means to be wrong about something, but their grammar errors are only 'wrong' if judged against Standard English.

If I say 3 + 2 makes 6, I have got it wrong. There is only one correct answer in mathematics to 3 + 2, and that is 5.

However, if I say, *'I's been to't' shops,'* that translates as *'I has been to the shops.'* In some areas, that would be correct for everyday chat and in literal translation of some languages into English, it might also be correct.

My local speak causes all the phonetic errors in the written form of the sentence, they reflect the points made about spelling through phonics. There is only one grammatical error in the sentence when it is compared with Standard English and that is *'I has'* which would be *'I have'*. However, in many dialects across the world this form is correct – it is not therefore 'wrong', it is different. More importantly, in many of the languages of other countries in the world, the construction they would use might translate this way – it is not therefore 'wrong' in translation either.

Many of us speak with a local accent that is correct grammatically, and some of us will occasionally slip a grammatical construction from the local dialect into our speech – especially when we are relaxed and chatting informally with people we know well – and it does not mean that we do not know what the standard form is. It certainly does not mean that we would do the same if speaking formally or writing.

These matters should be explained to the children in order to remove stigma from the way they speak and the way that translates into their writing. It is far more supportive and encouraging to say something like:

'Well done Lena, you said "I has been to the shops," and that is correct in the local accent you were speaking in. Now, do you know how we would say it in Standard English? (Pause) Does anyone know how we would say it in Standard English? Well done everyone, we would say, "I have been to the shops," and if we wished to shorten that we would say, "I've been to the shops." Please can we all say together: "I have been to the shops," and "I've been to the shops."'

This process should be repeated whenever needed and sometimes, when the teacher identifies that they are going to make deliberate changes in their speech in teaching about an aspect of the curriculum, these mismatches in the noun/verb form could be the common ones often heard in classrooms and seen in young children's writing.

Common examples of grammatical mismatches heard in speech and seen in writing in some communities include:

- *'We was...'*
- *'I is...'*
- *'Us has...'*
- *'Them does...'*
- *'You is...'*
- *'Him were...'*
- *'It be...'*
- *'I were...'*
- *'We is...'*
- *'Them has...'*

2. Dialects

Make children proud of our dialects!

Britain is home to a wide variety of dialects. Because travel was so slow, difficult, and rare prior to Victorian times, when the invention of railways started to change lives, most communities lived in almost total isolation with only the occasional horseman or carriage passing through. This meant that each locality developed its own form of the English language, both in vocabulary and in the structure of grammar. Where this has led to actual grammatical changes and new vocabulary that does not conform to Standard English, it is called dialect.

Some schools are located in areas where everyone born and bred there speaks in dialect. Children may grow up in homes where all they hear is dialect and they may not know there are alternative forms of speech, other than on the television or online.

Studying the various dialects represented in this book can help children to understand how language works. They can enjoy attempting to talk and read aloud in the different dialects, comparing the differences. It should be pointed out to them that the use of local accent at the same time also emphasises the dialect. Children all over the country who do not have a local accent will still be familiar with the Liverpool accent, Geordie (the North East), Birmingham, or London's cockney. They will certainly know the Scottish, Welsh, or Irish burr represented here, yet few people are familiar with all the various dialects.

The size and location of an area has a large impact on the number and spread of dialects. Yorkshire, for example, is the largest county in the country and has many variations in its dialect, whilst Scotland is a country where many rural and small-island communities were historically isolated and it too has many variations in patois.

Children aged four to six should have fun exploring different forms of speech orally. From the age of six upwards, the five codes of speech may be introduced through the study of examples, as explained below, and through using the many examples available from our website.

Activities

1. Discuss the meaning of the term dialect, using some short examples.

2. Spend short parts of lessons (around ten minutes) with everyone talking, discussing, and asking or answering questions in different speech codes. For example, when the children have met all the codes of speech, discussion in science today may be in our own local speak, in history tomorrow it may be in our class's own, unique dialect, and in English on Wednesday it may be in suave speak.

3. Read different dialects, trying to sound authentic – although they may be not be a true dialect.

4. Compare the structure of the language in two different dialects and play *spot the difference*.

5. Compare an example of the dialect with the same general meaning written in Standard English.

6. Identify how the dialect has changed the features of written English e.g. It doesn't use 't' on the end of words or it uses 't' instead of 'the'.

7. Translate sentences written in dialects into Standard English, orally and in writing.

8. Upgrade the Standard English version to suave speak by inserting suave features.

9. Put a dialect a day on the whiteboard, children re-write it in Standard English.

10. Create role play with one or more characters speaking in Standard English or in suave speak and one or more in a dialect.

11. Write stories containing direct speech with one or more characters speaking in dialect.

12. Ask children to explain the differences constantly between local accents, dialects, Standard English, and suave speak.

13. Create the class's own, unique dialect using borrowed language from other dialects and even their own made up code. You might name it after your teacher e.g. Jones Speak.

14. Work with children to translate short sections of direct speech in Standard English, taken from the class's own writing, class fiction, or passages created by the teacher, into the class's own dialect, making it fun.

15. Give children short passages written in the class dialect and ask them to turn them into Standard English.

16. Write and read short poems and verses in local speak and / or dialect, making it fun.

17. Ensure children become swift, confident code switchers, moving between Standard English, suave speak, and local speak.

Sample texts written in dialect are available *(see Chapter 10 - Games, Activities, and Examples)* and on our website.

The Variety of Our Dialects

Exemplar dialect forms of the same statement have been sent in from generous contributors from around the world. They are gratefully included here.

Original Statement

Hello, it is freezing cold out there.

Standard English Model

Hello, it is freezing cold out there. Come in and we'll have a cup of tea, and close that door.

Suave Speak Model

Good morning! Truly, it is bitterly cold outside. Do come along in and we shall secure the door. Perhaps we could enjoy a pleasant cup of tea together?

Dialect Models

Ay up me Duck; is freezin' in't i? Gerrin ear an'ahl mekk yerra brew.
Emma Turner, Leicester.

Alreyt? T'is proper cowd aht thee-er. Get in 'ere an' 'av a cup'a tea.
Danielle Hill, Sheffield, South Yorkshire.

Ah, t'is bare cold fam. Get in mi yard for some tea.
Dominic Lee, Somerset.

O'rite me mon. It ay arf cowd awt theya. Cum in an arl mek yow a cup o' tay.
Shirley Moffat, Black Country.

Alreet, 'tis frozen oot thayre. Hadaway in an' aal mek ye a cuppa.
Martin Bailey, Northumberland.

*Y'alreet Luvvy? T'is bloomin' baltic oot thur!
Ger'in an' we'll ger'a brew down yer neck.*
Cesca Astley, South Lancashire.

*Ayup! T'is brass monkeys aht theyre. Get
thissen in an' I'll put't' kettle on fer thee.*
Paul Garvey, Pontefract, West Yorkshire.

*Ayup! T'is baltic ahht there. Get yursen in
forra brew.*
Koren Sanderson, South Derbyshire.

*Alreyt! It's freezin' art theea. Gerrin en arl mek
thi a cuppa.*
Josh Wainwright, Barnsley, South Yorkshire.

*Watcha buh! Cood a'hell as 'tayters ewt
there. D'ya wat a cuppa?*
Nichola Ellen, Suffolk.

*A'right our kid? It's bloomin' cowd art there.
Cum in an' I'll mek a cuppa.*
Candace McColgan, Birmingham.

*Ay up, it's cord owt. Git yerssel in't'ous 'n'av a
cuppa tea.*
Sarah Gent, Northallerton, North Yorkshire.

*Y'awreet? It's frabs out der terday init? Wanna
come in an' ahl do yer a brew?*
Aaron Regan, Liverpool.

*Am yow gowin'? Yom froz oot there yow are!
Ged'in an oi'l mek yow a cuppa.*
KT Thompson, Black Country.

*A'rate duck, it's rate cowd owt there. Get
yersen inside an I'll mek thee a cuppa.*
Simon Kidwell, Stoke-on-Trent.

*Cum'in, put 't'wood in't'oyle an' we'll av
a brew!*
Mrs Horsy, Accrington.

*Awrigh? It's chankin' oot there. Ge' yersel' in
an' ah'll sor' ye oot wi' a cuppa.*
Lesley Davis, Kilmarnock, Ayrshire.

*Ayer Luv! 'S'freezing aht 'dere. Gerrin an' ah'll
stick't' kettle on!*
Kathryn Darwin, North East Liverpool.

*How pet, it's geet canny cald ootside. Gan
yersel in ferra brew man.*
Colin Grimes, North East.

*Awlroight borr, thas cowld owt thur, cum orn
in an oi'l mairk yew a brew.*
Tim Mycock, Norfolk.

*Whadda ya at? Some cold out dere... stay
where yous to an' I'll come where yer at an'
bring a cuppa tea an' a bickie.*
**Terry LaValley, Newfoundland and
Labrador, Canada.**

The footnote below, from Denise McCormick,
Northern Ireland, illustrates clearly the
complexities of allocating dialects to
locations and also some of the reasons there
are so many different forms of one dialect in
some areas.

*'My accent would be considered to be a
polite Northern Ireland accent... mind you
there are many different accents across
Northern Ireland. For instance, different
parts of County Londonderry have different
accents (e.g. Derry City is a completely
different accent to the more Scots sounding
Ballymena and Ballymoney accents).
Belfast is completely different again and
even different sections of the city of Belfast
have different accents. In the Newtownards
Peninsula area of County Down there can
be a mix of Scots sounding accents and
words used as there was a lot of mixing of
Scots people in that area (e.g. in the fishing
village of Portavogie, some people will
say yin and twa for one and two and the
village of Greyabbey is called Grabba by
the locals). Newry, on the border with the
Republic of Ireland, has people who sound
like they are from the Republic rather than
Northern Ireland. In fact, I know someone and*

you would swear they had been born and raised across the border but were born and raised in Newry. Northern Ireland has a wide diversity of local dialects which often isn't widely appreciated by anyone outside our little country, as people usually think we all sound either like the girls on Derry Girls or that all accents are like Belfast's (which is actually quite diverse as I said before). Just a 10 to 20-mile drive can lead to you speaking to people who sound like they are from another country. As I'm sure you are beginning to appreciate, it's a very complex business to say, 'What is your accent in Northern Ireland?'

3. Standard English

The use of Standard English should be justified in communities where it is rarely used, including for parents. This can be especially sensitive as, when launching the teaching and expectation for Standard English, some parents may receive the impression that it is because there is something 'wrong' with the way they speak. The way they speak is correct for life within the community where they live, and it can be crucial for esteem and integration. We should do our best to ensure people don't feel criticised.

In addition, it is not unusual for schools to consider asking for all parents to speak in Standard English at home, some of the time, with their children. This can cause tension on two counts. It can offend the parents and seem like the school is not valuing their home culture and their ethnicity, but it may also be that the parents themselves are not able to function comfortably in Standard English.

It is, therefore, vital that the school explains the importance of all children learning to talk and write in Standard English and to emphasise that if they are unable to think and speak in Standard English, they will be unable to write in it. Parents should be reassured that this does not mean that their children cannot still speak in their traditional ways at home and in the community, nor does it mean that they will ever have to learn to speak like the aristocracy. As long as their grammatical structures conform to Standard English, they may still have a local accent.

The Importance of Standard English

- Explain that writers, including authors, have to write books and articles in an agreed form of English that everyone will understand. It is like learning to drive a car – everyone has to conform to driving on the same agreed side of the road or there would be chaos. It does not necessarily mean that one side is better than the other side; in some countries people drive on the right, in Great Britain we drive on the left. It is just the agreed side, and as long as everyone knows which side it is and conforms to the rule, all is well. The agreed form of English for public communication is Standard English.
- Explain that the term Standard English means with the accepted grammatical structures.
- Explain that speaking in Standard English does not necessarily mean the speaker will not have a local accent, but they will not have a dialect. Briefly, explain what the difference is. A dialect may change grammatical structures and include words and phrases not heard in Standard English.
- Explain that many people speak in Standard English all the time at work e.g. teachers, doctors, newsreaders, and TV presenters (name some TV presenters

the children might know. You could even show children clips of the news).

- Point out the differences in the accents of staff in the school and others that pupils come into contact with, emphasising that they are all still mainly speaking in Standard English.

- Work with children to translate short sections of direct speech into Standard English. These may be taken from the class's own writing, class fiction, or passages created by the teacher. Change the examples into local speak if the latter has differences from Standard English, or use the class's own made up dialect, making it fun. Exemplar texts in dialect are available *(see Chapter 10 - Games, Activities, and Examples)*.

- Continue to repeat what a child says after the child has finished speaking publicly, slightly re-phrasing and correcting any grammar errors. Do not comment on the grammar errors.

- Teach all lessons in Standard English except when code switching in different lessons (possibly once a day). Expect all children to reply, discuss, and ask questions in Standard English except when asked to code switch. In the introduction to the lesson, the teacher may make a few deliberate mistakes in speech – children play *fastest shout first* to correct them. E.g.
Teacher: *Yesterday, we was watching...*
Child: *We were watching...*
Teacher: *Well done, Ben. Sorry, everyone. Yesterday, we were watching a video about the causes of the death of coral reefs. We talked about why the sea is getting warmer and also what things causes pollution...*
Child: *Things cause pollution...*
Teacher: *Well done, Asif. Sorry, everyone. What things cause pollution. Today we is...*
Child: *Today we are...*

Teacher: *Thank you, Maria. Sorry, everyone. Today we are going to...*

It is recommended that this is only sustained for a very short time, although the practice may be repeated once or twice a week, and the teacher may finally repeat it all in Standard English with no deviations, for emphasis.

4. Suave Speak

The adult activity described below should be executed in combination with the teaching of the five suave features *(see Chapter 4 - The 5 Suave Features of Language)*, and especially the use of suave words.

1. Encourage children to identify suave words when being read to, and praise them when they do. Use the context to identify or guess the meaning. Explain the meaning.

2. Play *the dictionary game*, if there is time, to see who can be fastest to find the word in the dictionary. The first child gives the page number and reads out the main definition.

3. Play the *thesaurus game*, if time, to see who can be fastest to find other words with the same or similar meaning in the thesaurus. The first child gives the page number and reads out two or more synonyms.

4. Play *make me up*, start making up sentences with some of the new, more sophisticated words in. These words should now be referred to as suave words.

5. Continue to spend part of a lesson or a session every day all talking in Standard English.

6. Introduce a suave word a week using suave word homework *(see Chapter 2 – Launching Talk:Write)* and use it in talk.

7. Play games using the suave word, including those named above and a wider range *(see Chapter 10 - Games, Activities, and Examples)*.

8. Demonstrate and practise selecting and inserting suave words into given sentences.

9. Remind children to use just a few suave words in a side of writing whenever they write for any purpose in any subject, saying too many can be as bad as none.

10. As children start to learn other suave features in talk and writing, expect them to use these features in both their public talk and their writing.

11. Play *fastest shout first* or *fastest finger first* when teaching, children have to shout out the word or shoot up their hand, if they hear you use a suave word in teaching.

12. Watch a recording of someone who speaks with received pronunciation – the accent of aristocrats in this country. Talk about how they speak differently to most of us. Practise talking with the accent of aristocrats for fun.

13. Explain that only about two percent of people in England actually speak like that all the time, but that we can do it for fun when we are speaking in suave speak, if we wish.

14. When children can speak in Standard English, sometimes with received pronunciation, and including suave features in their talk, they should receive a big celebration as they are now suave speakers.

15. Suave speakers are speaking the language of suave writers. The more they practise and the more confident they become in suave speak, the better they will write.

When children are ready, move on to the next stage.

Comparing Standard English and Local Speak

1. Write a sentence in local speak on the whiteboard. All read in local accent. E.g. *'Can yer sing Boss?' ('Can you sing, Sir?')*. Repeat several times with different sentences.

2. Translate orally into Standard English or confirm that it is already in Standard English.

3. Point out that local speak changes the spelling of some words when the writer spells them phonetically.

4. Model writing in Standard English below the local speak form, with correct spelling.

5. Children write in both forms if ready and able.

6. Talk together in pairs and small groups in local speak.

7. Compare the same sentences, both spoken and written, in Standard English and in local speak.

8. Start to talk together, as a class, in Standard English, if not already doing so.

9. Make it fun to spot when someone slips in to local speak during a Standard English speaking session.

10. Regularly ask children to switch between local speak and Standard English, and back.

11. Build up to all lessons being conducted in Standard English, unless told otherwise.

Code Switching: Local Speak to Standard English to Suave Speak and Back

Expect children to speak confidently in Standard English by age eight (providing they started Talk:Write by age five) whenever reminded to, and especially when answering questions in lessons (always in full, grammatically correct sentences) and in Talk:Write activities.

Play games and activities (including role play) that require children to switch easily and effortlessly between all three modes of language: local speak, Standard English and suave speak.

1. Tell children this combination of Standard English (grammatically correct English) and suave speak (speaking or writing with a selection of suave features) is their writer's voice and they are always to use it when they write, unless a character in their writing is speaking in local speak or dialect.

2. Expect children to always write grammatically correctly, using the suave features of writer's voice when appropriate.

3. From age nine and above, expect all children (unless new to school) to model code switching with confidence and to make oral presentations in suave speak to their class, other classes, and in school assemblies.

5. Writer's Voice

When the majority or all of the class have a thorough understanding of the differences between the local accents, dialects, and the daily speech forms of their area, plus the reasons why we all need to be completely fluent and confident in Standard English for speaking and writing – even if it is different from the speech of our communities – we introduce the aspect of writer's voice, explaining that many writers across the world write in forms and styles of 'voice' that are quite different from their own daily voice. This is usually for one of three reasons:

- They are conforming to the rules of Standard English so that their work can be widely understood.
- They are changing their voice for the speech of various characters who may be very young, very old, or come from different places.
- They are enriching their daily language for the purpose of writing.

The writer may, in fact, be thinking and composing with a local accent as they write, but that will not change the accuracy of the standard form of grammar, as long as no dialect forms of grammar creep in. Neither should it distort spelling providing the school is implementing an effective spelling policy with children from an early age. It should now be explained to the class that we are working to develop our own, personal writer's voice.

Use the following types of activity to explain the concept of writer's voice as it was interpreted historically. Point out that many of the sentence structures of our traditional tales and nursery rhymes are not in use in modern literature.

Identifying Writer's Voice in Well-Known Rhymes

1. Choose class stories or rhymes that use more sophisticated language, focus on the difference between the writer's voice in these and our

daily talk. Ask children how we would normally say the same thing in our daily chat.

2. Ask children to recite a known nursery rhyme. Scribe the relevant part on the whiteboard.

3. Can the children detect any parts where the wording or sequence of words is quite different to the way any of us speak today?

4. Explain that historically, most nursery rhymes and traditional stories were never written down. They were repeated by word of mouth from one family to another and from one community to another. They were told, therefore, in the traditional language structures of the time. People who originally made up these rhymes and tales used the most sophisticated forms of language they knew. In some schools, it may be appropriate for older children to look at the language in original religious scripts, including The Bible and the Koran, and classical tales.

5. Children discuss how the language is different from the structures of daily speech today, whether that is Standard English or local speak. E.g.
   - *'There came a big spider...'* – *'A big spider came...'* (Little Miss Muffet)
   - *'And Jill came tumbling after!'* – *'And Jill fell down after...'* (Jack and Jill)
   - *'Down came the raindrops...'* – *'The raindrops came down...'* (Incey Wincey Spider)
   - *'Did ever you see such a thing in your life?'* – *'Did you ever see such a thing in your life?'* (Three Blind Mice)
   - *'Four and twenty blackbirds baked in a pie.'* – *'24 blackbirds baked in a pie.'* (Sing a Song of Sixpence)

6. Explain that these more elaborate written features of English are known as writer's voice.

7. From this point, acknowledge writer's voice when reading stories and poems to or with the class.

It should now be explained to the class that we are aiming to develop our own writer's voice that we can use whenever we write in school. This will not use historic forms, but it will sometimes be different from our daily speaking voice. Our writer's voice will be composed of:
- writing that is in technically correct Standard English.
- writing that has sophisticated words and phrases that we do not normally use in daily speech (suave features).

> Explain that we have a new word for 'sophisticated' and that is **suave**.

From now on, all sophisticated words will be called suave words and other sophisticated features in writing will be called suave features. In order to become totally confident about writing in our emergent writer's voice, we are going to speak in it. This will be our new, very sophisticated language and we shall call it suave speak.

Respect for All

Most countries of the world now have diverse communities settled in juxtaposition within the same locality. Some communities integrate naturally with others, sharing elements of their cultures and languages, while others cherish their personal identity within the locality, maintaining their home culture and languages, which they continue to use in their daily life. Migration from the furthest corners of a country into the cities and urban localities with a potential for employment and income generation is widespread, as is migration between countries and across continents.

The coming of industry to countries around the world, however, drew populations to cluster around ports, cities, and other industrial areas, mingling with the incoming populations from overseas. Many variants of accents and dialects resulted from this integration. Migrants who did not share the language of the host country would learn their own form of this new language, creating a mix of local accents and adapted dialects. The result is that in many countries, including those of Great Britain, there are huge variations in the versions of English heard on the streets and lanes.

New residents arriving in England, and also children growing up in communities where the home language remains the language for daily use within the home and its immediate surroundings, learn an adapted form of the host language without always knowing that this variant does not conform to the rules and forms of Standard English. Thus, there has emerged a pattern of peoples speaking in various accents, dialects, patois, and adapted street talk.

None of these forms of speech are wrong; they are purely different. However, historically, an agreed set of rules for construction of sentences, consistent use of punctuation, and accurate use of spelling patterns that – in English at least – rarely follow the precise codes of phonics, has been embedded and accepted as the code of universal communication in English – whether in speech or in writing – and has become known as Standard English. In order to succeed in employment, travel, or communication across communities, localities, and countries, it is necessary to learn the code of Standard English.

> This is not because Standard English is 'right' or 'better' than all the other varied speech codes, but because it is the one that is widely understood and accepted.

It is the responsibility of schools to ensure that all children are able to talk confidently in Standard English whilst protecting their own local speech codes, dialects, and languages. Children will learn to switch into accurate Standard English through talk, through talking about talk, and through practising switching between the different forms or codes of talk that they hear.

Children will learn to write in Standard English through learning to speak in Standard English.

If a child can say it, a child can write it!

> If a child can say it in Standard English, a child can write it in Standard English!

Thus, we – as teachers – are working in an area of high sensitivity. We could be at risk of seeming to criticise or challenge the way children in our schools, their parents, and their communities speak. This must not happen. The way they speak is likely to be correct for the community in which they live and is certainly correct for communication within the family of which they are a part. It is vital, therefore, that all references to local accents and dialects are made with the greatest respect.

We believe that the Talk:Write approach should create an atmosphere within school that makes attempting dialects and accents a fun and inclusive activity. We hope that it has the effect of bringing children together and promoting the celebration of difference.

However, if you feel that attempting dialects or accents is not right for your setting, that is understandable. You can still make use of the activities available, with appropriate adjustments.

We feel it is necessary, as a final note to the section on the use of English, to acknowledge that elements leading to English being widely used around the world were, and are, very harmful. Issues such as slavery, colonisation, and imperialism had major roles in spreading the English language. These issues are beyond the scope of this book, but we strongly encourage your school to be aware and to be teaching these issues in full context.

Chapter 4 – The 5 Suave Features of Language

Analysis of children's writing shows that there are five suave features of language that enrich the writer's voice, increase atmosphere, enhance description, and improve the reading experience. These features are easy to learn and can be used effectively by children from the age of six upwards. In the Talk:Write process they are taught through simple, fun activities and games that children enjoy.

The 5 Suave Features of Language

1. **Suave Words:** Words that are sophisticated for the age of the child. They might make the reader think, *'Fancy a child of this age knowing that word.'*

2. **Suave Sentence Openers:** Children learn to use a wide range of features of language to open sentences that make openings more interesting or varied, for example linking and sequence words, 'ly' words (adverbs), 'ing' words (gerunds), and connectives.

3. **Suave Connectives:** Connectives may be defined as conjunctions, prepositions, and adverbs that join, link, or extend phrases and sentences. There are a very large number of connectives and by using a variety, including some of the more sophisticated ones, children's writing is greatly enhanced. (The word connectives is an umbrella term given in dictionaries such as the Concise Oxford Dictionary).

4. **Suave Punctuation:** A range of punctuation supports the reader in interpreting the text. All punctuation is important and should be taught, but in Talk:Write there is a particular focus on punctuation that lifts the pace of writing:
   - Age 6 to 8: ? ! …
   - Age 8 to 12: ? ! … " " () –

5. **Literary Features:** There are a range of literary features that enrich writer's voice and enhance style e.g. alliteration, simile, metaphor, onomatopoeia, personification, figurative language, and passive voice.

Start to introduce the wider range of features for Talk:Write in ways that work best with your curriculum, and repeatedly use the new examples in games and activities across the curriculum.

For games, activities, and examples of a weekly plan of sessions *(see Chapter 10 - Games, Activities, and Examples).*

Teaching and Embedding Suave Features

Suave features will need to be taught to the majority of pupils in a school, as they are not usual features of daily language for most children, and to be embedded through their frequent use, both in oral games and activities and in writing.

Older pupils will be able to cope with the introduction of suave features much sooner than younger children, probably within two weeks of meeting Talk:Write or as soon as they have grasped the differences in the way people talk and the importance of the writer's voice. Younger pupils may need a few weeks to just explore different ways of talking but should be ready after the first half term at the latest.

Once children are speaking in Standard English with confidence, it is the inclusion of suave features of language that secures the speech as suave speak. When children write in Standard English, including suave features in their writing, this becomes their writer's voice.

The first feature to be introduced should always be suave words, as many of the other features are composed of words that could fall into this category. Initially, the class will have sufficient examples of suave words (which some may call sophisticated or 'posh' words) between them to introduce suave speaking into the code-switching process, but as soon as they are secure in that process the pro-active teaching of a wide range of suave features should commence.

The following is the approach for this process, which then becomes ongoing with the challenge level increasing as the children mature.

The introduction to Talk:Write includes examining and trailing different codes of speech and starting to learn to code switch from one code to another with ease. This process is then examined in detail *(see Chapter 3 – The 5 Codes of Speech).* Sessions are then devised that enable children to practise these skills through enjoyable activities.

Remember the research: it can take up to 12 exposures to embed a new word, to fully understand it, and to use it correctly. The more activities we enjoy using new features of language, and the more contexts we use them in across the curriculum, the better children will learn and understand them.

Enjoyment is a key part of the Talk:Write process, as children who are having fun are alert and attentive, and thus learn more easily. They also retain their learning better – the humour acts as a trigger to remember the content. This is why much of the embedding of new vocabulary takes place through fun activities that we call games.

The following stages build on from the focus on the different ways people speak.

1. Suave Words

Suave words are words that are sophisticated for a child of the age being taught; words that they would not normally know or use. These are the type of words that may appear in some reading books, stories, or novels, but many children will 'jump' over them rather than tackling them, and – even if they do read them – many children will forget them almost immediately.

They may be almost any part of speech e.g. nouns, adjectives, adverbs, verbs, or connectives within sentences.

Most children will be learning at least one new suave word a week through suave word homework *(see Chapter 2 - Launching Talk:Write)*, when Talk:Write is implemented effectively. This presents an additional challenge in that many suave words are also hard to spell, and applying rules of phonics to more complex suave words rarely works. It is for this reason that all children might be taught the five 'S' system for spelling *(see Chapter 5 - The 5 'S' System for Spelling)* if their existing spelling strategies are not effective for complex suave words.

Introduce one word at a time. Determine they know the meaning through use of illustrations or mimes, use the word in meaningful sentences, and play games such as the *dictionary/thesaurus game* (if there is sufficient time), then make up simple sentences with it in.

1. Write the target word on the whiteboard, all read it together, explain the meaning.
2. Use the word in sentences to model its use.
3. If it has more than one meaning, explain this and explain which meaning the class are using it for that day.
4. Use the five 'S' system for spelling to learn to spell the word and to further embed it.
5. Play games involving the word.
6. Use the word yourself, regularly and across the curriculum. Ask children to shoot hands up if they hear you use the word, or to shout it out *('Let's play fastest shout first or fastest finger first')* after you stop speaking.

7. Create opportunities for natural use of the word within the teaching of a range of subjects across the curriculum.
8. When children truly know and understand a new word, which may be in as little as a week for some children and may be two or three weeks for other children, some will start to use the word quite naturally. For others, it is helpful to prompt them, saying something like: *'Please remember to use a few suave words – and wouldn't it be exciting if someone used our new word?'*
9. Praise / reward a child who uses the word in speech or writing without being prompted.
10. As a suave word becomes embedded, a new example should be introduced, so that the repertoire is constantly widening. As many as possible of the children's new words should be incorporated into games and activities *(see Chapter 10 - Games, Activities, and Examples)*.
11. Sometimes, give each child or pair of children their own special suave word to learn and use. Ask them to make up a sentence with it in, so that other class members can guess what their word means. Within one term (or less) most children should be writing at length with a good range of suave words in their writing.

Remember: most children do not retain and fully understand how to use a new word after meeting it once. They need to use it repeatedly over a number of sessions, for some it may be up to 12, in different contexts and in different ways. The games and activities for Talk:Write are perfect for this when applied across the curriculum.

All children do not have to retain and use all words as long as they are all acquiring a good repertoire. In fact, it is useful when different children remember and use different words – that is what happens in 'real life'.

Exemplar Suave Words

The following lists are only examples, and the age bands are only guidance. Some younger children may be using words that are far more sophisticated than some older pupils. This is helpful as they prove to be role models and active contributors in games and activities – and in the celebration of the outcomes in actual writing.

The illustration of a progression in the challenge level of the examples is also only for exemplification. Different children may be at different points with regards to more sophisticated forms of the same root word. None of this should be a deterrent and all words are good for playing with and talking about. Different children will use different forms in different contexts – that is how it is in real life and that is how it should be.

Age 4 to 6

- flower
- teacher
- car
- said
- clothes
- run
- nice
- nasty
- pretty
- cross

Age 6 to 8

- plant
- instructor
- motorcar
- spoke
- clothing
- race
- kind
- unkind
- attractive
- angry

Age 8 to 10

- herb
- educator
- vehicle
- announced
- garments
- sprint
- kindly
- cruel
- stunning
- furious

Age 10 to 12

- vegetation
- educationalist
- transportation
- articulated
- apparel
- hastened
- benevolent
- malevolent
- scintillating
- irate

2. Suave Sentence Openers

The following exemplar suave sentence openers are not presented by age band, but rather in a slight progression of challenge from top to bottom. A suave sentence opener may not necessarily be a sophisticated word in its own right, it is the use of it to open a sentence that is powerful.

Only expect children to use suave sentence openers formed from words they already know and can spell. If it is necessary for them to learn a new one that is unknown, use the five 'S' system for spelling.

Exemplar Suave Sentence Openers

Time

- Today...
- Yesterday...
- Last month...
- Next week...
- At midday...
- At nine o'clock...
- Before supper...
- In the night...
- During the week of...

Sequence

- First...
- Then...
- Next...
- Last...
- Finally...

- In the end...
- Before...
- After...
- A little while later...

'ly' openers (fronted adverbials)

- Slowly...
- Rapidly...
- Fortunately...
- Anxiously...
- Frequently...
- Surreptitiously...
- Morosely...

'ing' openers (gerunds)

- Walking...
- Hoping...
- Wishing...
- Thinking...
- Anticipating...
- Devouring...
- Ruminating...

Connectives

- Because...
- If...
- When...
- Also...
- Although...
- Despite...
- Contrary to...

3. Suave Connectives

It does not matter whether a connective is actually an adverb, a preposition, or a conjunction, from the point of view of writing. As long as the word or phrase is appropriate for extending or joining sentences and as long as it sounds 'right' in the sentence and enhances the flow or quality of writing, then it is good for the purpose.

When introducing previously unknown higher challenge connectives, you may use the five 'S' system for spelling.

Exemplar Suave Connectives

The following are exemplification only and a child may know and be using examples from different stages at the same age.

Age 4 to 6

- and
- but
- so
- because

Age 6 to 8

- plus
- yet
- then
- as

Age 8 to 10

- also
- however
- thus
- as a result of

Age 10 to 12

- additionally
- despite
- consequently
- due to

4. Suave Punctuation

There is a natural progression in understanding and using sentence punctuation for most children, and there is no doubt that reading excerpts from texts, particularly when done out loud, can be a great help in clarifying its purpose and use. Reading a punctuated paragraph together as a group or class, moving punctuation around, or changing punctuation can be fun activities, and also a meaningful learning experience for young children. Inserting punctuation into an unpunctuated paragraph *(for Bud's Work, see page 98)* can also be enjoyable.

The Punctuation Pyramid is still available online and is useful as a classroom display.

The following pieces of punctuation may be classified as suave punctuation because of the sophistication they bring to the construction of sentences. Some higher-challenge levels of punctuation have been omitted (e.g. the apostrophe and the colon) not because they are not important – they are extremely important and children should learn to use them accurately – but because they do not have the same immediate impact on the flow or expressive quality of text for the reader.

Exemplar Suave Punctuation

Age 4 to 6

Will be learning the full stop, capital letter, and comma.

Suave punctuation:

- **?** as in questions.
- **!** as in exclamations.
- **...** as in ellipsis.

Age 6 to 8

Will be learning the full stop, capital letter, comma, question mark, exclamation mark, and ellipsis.

Suave punctuation:

- **" "** as in direct speech.
- **–** as in dash instead of a comma.

Age 8 to 10

Will be learning the full stop, capital letter, comma, question mark, exclamation mark, ellipsis, speech marks, and dash.

Suave punctuation:

- **( )** as in an aside.
- **;** as in semi-colon instead of a full stop or connective.

Age 10 to 12

Will be learning the full stop, capital letter, comma, question mark, exclamation mark, ellipsis, speech marks, dash, brackets, and semi-colon.

Suave punctuation:

- **, , – – ( )** as in double commas, double dashes, and brackets for parenthesis.
- **; :** as in semi-colon and colon for division.

5. Literary Features

Literary features have unique expressive qualities that add colour or power to a child's writing. They have been organised in a recommended sequence for teaching.

Exemplar Literary Features

Age 6 to 8

- **Alliteration:** repeated use of the same letter to start words in a phrase. E.g. The sad, sleepy snail...

Age 8 to 10

Will be learning alliteration.

- **Personification:** talking about something as though it was something else or had the skills of something else. E.g. The car brakes squealed as it... The wind cut through the...
- **Simile:** compares two things that are not alike, using as, like, or than. E.g. She is as old as the hills. He croaked like a frog. Her eyes were brighter than the stars.
- **Onomatopoeia:** use of a word that makes the same or similar sound as its meaning. E.g. boom, crash, whisper, plop. Water gurgled in the pipe.

Age 10 to 12

Will be learning alliteration, personification, simile, and onomatopoeia.

- **Metaphor:** uses the pairing of two things that are not alike without using as, like, or than. E.g. Her velvet skin... The galloping clouds... With eyes of ice, he stared...
- **Passive Voice:** the object of a sentence becomes the subject. It may often be followed by 'by'. E.g. The cake was eaten by the dog. The path was flooded by the storm. The whole village was struck down ('by flu' might be understood from the context within the story e.g. already knowing there was a flu epidemic).

Once the concept of people speaking and writing in different voices is clear and well understood, the class is ready to start enjoying the games and activities that are the staple diet of Talk:Write.

Differentiation by Pitch and Expectation

Suave words are words that would be ambitious for a child of that age but that are within their intellectual grasp. This works equally well for mixed-age classes as it does for single-aged classes, as it is the child's age that influences the judgement. Thus, no differentiation is needed other than:

- The pitch of the word i.e. the degree of challenge for the age of the child.
- The amount of time expected between starting to learn the word, starting to try to use it in either speech or writing – although they may make mistakes – and being able to use it accurately and effectively in both speech and writing.

Over-Use of Suave Features

Initial over-use of suave features is normal and should not be seen as a weakness. Early suave speak and the child's emergent writer's voice may be littered with suave words, some of them used incorrectly, or almost every sentence may have a suave sentence opener. Praise the child for 'trying to use' suave features and then – at a slightly different time – show fictitious examples of children's work *(for Bud's Work, see page 98)* with over-use and explain that using too many can be as wrong as not using any.

> Do not be discouraged by misuse – and do not allow children to be.

Do remember that when first learning a new process in mathematics e.g. long multiplication, most children make mistakes and some children struggle for a long time, but teachers do not give up. It is the same with features of talk and writing.

Planning and presenting paragraphs written in writer's voice and read out in suave speak is an excellent way of supporting children in learning to manage their new skills, making them more effective.

Give children simple rules for limitation, if needed:

1. Please do not use more than two suave words in a paragraph of writing or talk.
2. Please do not use more than one suave sentence opener in a paragraph of writing or talk.
3. Please do not use one sort of suave punctuation more than once in a paragraph of writing or talk.
4. Please do not use more than one literary feature in a paragraph of writing or talk.

When children have learnt control, tell them that some rules are there to be broken and if the writing would be improved by using more than one or two examples in a paragraph, they should do it, e.g. a repeated use of a question mark such as: *'Where was he? Why hadn't he come? Could something terrible have happened to him?'*

Maintaining Best Practice in Talk:Write

Once Talk:Write has been introduced, it follows a similar pattern throughout the years of primary education, that is that four times a week a class will play games and complete activities that focus on suave speak. Once a week, they will have a short session immediately prior to the suave writing session that includes five minutes of refresher games featuring newly learnt language followed by ten minutes of individual planning time.

Children will then spend up to 50 minutes producing a piece of extended, unsupported writing using some of the new features they have learnt. However, teachers should have the same high expectation for the quality of writing whenever they ask the class to write something. Whether this is a passage in the humanities or a report in science, all children should be expected to use their highest standard of writing skills, including their developing writer's voice.

> There should now be a rule in every classroom that there will no longer be any 'sloppy' writing – all writing is 'best' writing.

This expectation will lead to the re-programming of the children's brains so that high quality writing is produced automatically every time there is a task to be done.

Chapter 5 – The 5 'S' System for Spelling

Spelling approaches are often complicated in the English language as so many words do not conform to the rules of phonics. There are so many different ways of spelling the same sound e.g. 'ff' as in fluff, 'ough' as in rough, 'ough' as in cough, and 'euph' as in euphoria. This is further compounded by the same spelling patterns seeming to make different or no sounds in other words e.g. 'ough' as in through and 'uph' as in upheld.

Ricketts, Dawson, and Davies state:

In emphasising the importance of orthography as well as phonology and semantics in lexical representations, the lexical quality hypothesis (Perfetti & Hart, 2002) is consistent with the prediction that orthographic facilitation will occur in word learning.

Buried in this treasure of academia is the research findings of the additional difficulty that codes of speech can have on the spelling of words when attempting to apply the rules of phonics, and the premise that if teaching of new words is backed up by the visual and conventional spelling of the word, as well as sounds and meaning, children learn and retain the word so much better.

Moreover, whilst spoken and written representations of language vary across contexts as a result of changes in voice, accent, handwriting, font, and so on, arguably, this is more pronounced for speech. Therefore, orthographic forms may be more readily learned than phonological forms, providing a more effective anchoring device, or hook, on which to hang semantic information.

The Hidden Depths of New Word Knowledge: Using graded measures of orthographic and semantic learning to measure vocabulary acquisition (Ricketts, Dawson, and Davies, 2021).

This research is reflected in the development of the five 'S' system for spelling; a highly effective system for learning the spelling of complex, non-conforming vocabulary.

The spelling system has five features:

1. **See:** Look at the word; see its shape and length.
2. **Say:** Say the word loudly and clearly as a group.
3. **Spell:** Spell the word by letter names loudly, clearly, and all together, **and at the same time:**
4. **Scribe:** 'Write' the letters with the bare fingertip as they are said.
5. **Solve:** Say the agreed meaning together.

Repetition is key to the process. Steps two to five are repeated three times. Each repetition of scribe uses a different surface:

1. Bare fingertip on a table top.
2. Bare fingertip on a fabric surface e.g. sleeve or shoulder.
3. Bare fingertip on flesh e.g. forearm, back of the hand, or forehead.

This system is easy to implement and highly effective, but it depends on a brisk pace and commitment to the sequence of the features as they are intended. It can work alongside other programmes for teaching the skills of spelling or writing, or it can be implemented in part. It can work well alongside a school's programme for teaching phonics and may be used only for more complex spellings or for the weekly suave words.

Word pronunciation changes over time, with the written form of a word often failing to keep up. There are also large variations in pronunciation and spelling caused by varying accents and dialects. Added to this, the orthography (rules surrounding the construction and composition of writing) can be irregular, which makes predicting pronunciation or spelling difficult.

> **"**
>
> *Some teachers and education source books use the terms 'high frequency words' and 'sight words' synonymously. However, they are not the same. High frequency words can be phonetically regular, meaning that they can be blended and/or segmented. They are those words which occur frequently in reading and writing. Juxtaposed to this, sight words cannot be easily blended and/or segmented and need to be recognised on sight.*
>
> **Let's Look at Spelling (Dr Lorraine Beveridge and Jane Lieschke, 2017)**

High frequency words and sight words together make up around half the words that children will meet in texts, and thus need explicit teaching alongside the teaching of the names of letters, the sounds made by individual letters, the meaning of all words taught, and the school's programme for phonics. In *The Role of Orthographic Mapping in Learning to Read* (2020), Joan Sedita says that the average adult may have between 30,000 and 60,000 words in their sight vocabulary, and that as soon as one of these words is seen in text it is instantly and unconsciously recognised. This is the ability that enables us to become efficient readers, able to focus on the meaning of text rather than decoding words.

The five 'S' system for spelling requires the learner to deploy their senses of sight, speech, hearing, and touch all at the same time. This has the maximum impact possible on the sensory system, transmitting the information to the brain and embedding it. Not all children have the full function of all senses, so the system provides multi-sensory support for the spelling process. The learning of a new and complex word through the five 'S' system for spelling may require repetition of the process four or five times within the week for some children, by which time the word and its correct spelling should be secure. As the system itself has repetition of three times built in, this will give each child the optimum number of experiences (12 in total) through which to learn the word. This system works perfectly with the learning of one or two new suave words each week to enrich pupils' vocabulary and enhance their writing.

Spelling a New Suave Word

The example word is 'strode'.

1. See

- Look at the word 'strode' together on the whiteboard, flipchart, or flashcard. Can anyone 'read' it already? Does anyone know what it means?
- The teacher writes or says 'strode' in the context of simple, relevant sentences that give clues. Can anyone guess the meaning of the word now?
- Play *fastest finger first* (if time) to find 'strode' in a dictionary or a thesaurus. Discuss the meaning and identify known synonyms.
- Read a simple sentence that uses 'strode' and gives a clue to the meaning.

  Nimo strode down the street, eager to reach the shop.

  The teacher strode angrily into the classroom.

- The teacher asks if anyone can guess what 'strode' might mean? The teacher then tells the class the meaning, using as simple a form as possible, preferably with only one or two words in the meaning. This is not always possible. The word 'strode' means walked quickly with big steps.
- Discuss the meaning with each other. As a class, agree the meaning.
- The teacher models, then all children stride round the room.

2. Say

- Say the word clearly – 'strode'.

3. Spell

- Spell the word (by alphabet name), 's t r o d e', **while at the same time,**

4. Scribe

- Write 'strode' with the naked tip of the key writing finger (usually the first finger of the right or left hand) on a **smooth surface** such as the tabletop or a smooth book cover.

5. Solve

- Solve the meaning together. Agree a final, clear and simple definition as a class and say the meaning together at the end. The word 'strode' means walked quickly with big steps.

Repeat a second time.

2. Say

- Say the word clearly – 'strode'.

3. Spell

- Spell the word (by alphabet name), 's t r o d e', **while at the same time,**

4. Scribe

- Write 'strode' with the naked tip of the key writing finger on the **textured surface** of part of own clothing e.g. the opposite sleeve or shoulder.

5. Solve

- Solve the meaning together.

Repeat a third time.

2. Say

- Say the word clearly – 'strode'.

3. Spell

- Spell the word (by alphabet name), 's t r o d e', **while at the same time,**

4. Scribe

- Write 'strode' with the naked tip of the key writing finger on **bare skin** e.g. back of own hand, forearm, or on the forehead.

5. Solve

- Solve the meaning together.

Finally

- Say the word and meaning again.
- Play *make me up* to create sentences in twos that use the word 'strode' correctly.
- Feedback to the whole class.

> Repeat all the above at least four more times that week.

> Encourage children to use the word in appropriate contexts, including in lessons across the curriculum, playing *make me up*, and in as many ways as possible.

Chapter 6 – The Suave Writing Session

All children should be taking part in a silent, unsupported writing session once a week every week after it has been established in a class; writing is far too important and complex a process to leave it for longer. Just as mathematics is taught through carefully planned programmes that introduce a new skill, practise it, and embed it, teach accurate writer's voice thoroughly and then provide a period of 'bedding in' for accuracy and retention. Teaching the features and skills of writer's voice must be given the same commitment as is given for other key skills in learning.

Children need opportunity to repeat and embed all their emerging skills as writers, including the features of Talk:Write. They need to continually practise and develop their creativity, their basic skills, and their ability to respond accurately to the stimulus. Furthermore, they need regular opportunity to demonstrate the impact of the Talk:Write process on their developing writer's voice and style. Finally, they need to build stamina as writers... the ability to sustain the process of writing for prolonged periods of time as they grow older *(see Chapter 7 - Stamina with Style)*.

These weekly, silent writing sessions are called suave writing sessions.

Suave writing sessions are not for teaching the skills of writing. The teaching of skills is done in timetabled English lessons and – in the case of suave speak activities to embed new language features – across the curriculum and in the four flexible short sessions a week.

All the progression steps for developing writer's voice and style *(see Chapter 8 - Progress Steps for Composition)* should be introduced in planned lessons and then can be worked into short activities or games for the 10 to 15-minute Talk:Write slots across the curriculum throughout each week *(see Chapter 10 - Games, Activities, and Examples)*.

An exemplar timetable for the suave writing session is provided for reference *(see Chapter 2 - Launching Talk:Write)*.

Why Are Some Children Reluctant to Write?

There are four main reasons why some children are reluctant writers:

1. **Verbal barriers to success:** Some pupils do not have the range of vocabulary or linguistic confidence to write and fear that they will fail. Pupils

with English as an additional language (EAL) in the earlier stages of learning English, some children with disabilities, and children not exposed to enough talk or reading in their first four years of life may fall into this bracket. It is important to remember that older children with EAL may actually be very effective writers in first (or 'home') language, even though they are not yet able to transfer their literary skills into English.

Answer: Teach new language through Talk:Write; build high quality, planned talk into lessons across the curriculum, and deploy the best practice in teaching children new to English how to speak and write in English.

2. **Life barriers to success:** Some pupils feel they have too little experience of life and the world, and feel they have nothing relevant to say. Children raised in isolation or in isolated, small communities may fall into this bracket. Also, children who spend too much time on technology learn to rely on the ideas and the creativity of others to fill their time. Some children have rich life experiences but they may not include the type of activities that are generally celebrated in writing stimuli in the school they are in.

Answer: Deploy all tactics as in the answer to point one, whilst also exposing the child to a wide range of stimulating pictures, short videos, stories, etc. to widen secondary experiences. Use known direct experiences from the children's daily lives at home and in school in the past as stimuli. Plan as many field trips and real experiences into the curriculum as possible. Always invest time in pre-planning and exposure prior to asking these pupils to write in the early stages. Develop imagination – take walks in the 'jungle', across the 'desert', and up the 'mountain' outside and in the hall, playing appropriate music and with vocal description through a speaker. Describe… describe… describe!

3. **Physical barriers to success:** Some pupils feel that writing is exhausting and makes their wrist and hand muscles ache. They find it very difficult to sustain the process of writing for long enough to finish a side of A4 or more at one sitting.

Answer: Exercise the 'writing' hand and arm to build physical stamina over several weeks. Develop fun exercise routines to popular tunes.

4. **Social barriers to success:** Some pupils feel they can't write and would rather avoid it than be seen to fail. Some children might be described as systemisers; the systemiser needs to analyse and understand the system and be able to replicate or complete it if possible. These children prefer to work to guidelines and structures. Other children are more inclined towards being empathisers; they need to understand how people can be best pleased and to achieve that if possible. When they understand the outcome the teacher is seeking, they strive to achieve it.

Answer: Talk:Write gives systemisers a system for writing with steps and a structure that they can understand and replicate, thus leading to success. It gives empathisers a framework for success that will please the teacher and others. Thus, everyone can succeed within the system.

How to Re-Motivate the De-Motivated Writer

1. Don't write at length for the first two to three weeks, but do write the parts of a whole piece (e.g. the opening, the body, or the ending) in different subjects across the curriculum. E.g. say things like: *'I would like you to spend the next X minutes of our geography lesson planning and writing the opening to a factual report on glaciers,'* or *'Please spend the next X minutes writing instructions for how to make a model crane with moving parts,'* or *'You now have X minutes to write the closing paragraph of a report about endangered animals.'*

2. Select two fiction titles for writing that will be done in the next suave writing session (in three weeks) that will interest and engage your pupils. Make them relevant to the life and school experiences all children in the class have and/or the books, TV, games they enjoy. Forget the curriculum for now, unless something you are studying has particularly excited them. Examples of relevant titles accessible by children with limited or different life experiences for school stimuli might be: 'The Day I Met an Alien in the School Hall' or 'The Day I Bought Magic Melons from Our Market'

3. In the suave writing session for week one, the titles are discussed in parts of two separate English lessons:

    -   Images of aliens are examined and discussed. What are they? Where might they be from? How might they arrive? What might they want?

    -   Aliens may be drawn, discussed, and described in one 15-minute Talk:Write session. Collect describing words for aliens.

    -   Melons are examined, discussed, described, tasted.

    -   The market is discussed, described, role played. Photographs are examined.

    -   The subject of magic is discussed. Examples of what magic could do are explored. What might happen if you ate a piece of magic melon?

    -   Children write an opening for one of the titles – chosen by the child. The teacher prompts them to identify at least two characters, a setting, when it all started, and so on. Children use the LDD approach *(see Chapter 7 - Stamina with Style)* to enrich their opening with four or five facts. The teacher prompts them to add a detailed description of at least one character and the setting.

    -   When writing these pieces over a number of weeks, it is useful to ensure the pupils can see the previously completed sections and to give them a little time to refresh themselves on what they have already written.

4. In the suave writing session for week two, children write the body for their chosen title. The teacher prompts them to identify at least one new character, a change in setting, what happened, and so on. The teacher prompts them to add detailed description of at least one character and of something that happened in the body. Children use the LDD approach to enrich the body of their writing.

5. In the suave writing session for week three, children write an ending for their chosen title. The teacher prompts them to identify at least two characters who are important at the end, a final setting, how it all ended, and so on. The teacher prompts them to add a description of the thoughts and

feelings of at least one character, and a description of something else. Children use the LDD approach to enrich the ending of their writing.

6. Examples of openings, bodies, and endings are shared as a class as the days pass. The teacher and class members make suggestions for insertions and additions.

7. Spend significant time in talk around the titles of choice, one title at a time, identifying words and phrases that are relevant, and discussing possible alternative storylines, developments, and ideas. Collect powerful words and phrases on the wall.

8. Play games around *make me up* for sentences about things you are learning across the curriculum and the two writing titles you are working on. Sometimes say, *'Make me up a sentence with X in it'* (a powerful adjective, adverb, or verb) or, *'Make me up a sentence that starts with X'* (a powerful opening such as an 'ly' word / an adverb – slowly, happily, anxiously, or an 'ing' word / a gerund – hoping, hurrying, thinking, etc.). Usually choose generic suave words and phrases that would work for either title.

9. The day before your first planned, extended, and unsupported writing session, put the two titles on the whiteboard and give pupils time to discuss in twos or threes before asking them to make a final choice. Build up the anticipation and make it sound and feel exciting. Talk about all the wonderful ideas, words, and phrases they have worked on. Give them time to gather in a group by each of the titles chosen, to refresh their ideas.

10. Introduce and explain suave writing homework *(see Chapter 2 - Launching Talk:Write)*, if this has not already been done.

11. Make the silent writing session the next day as special and exciting as possible by following the advice in this chapter.

12. Use the LDD cards for length through detail and description to prompt the children into adding the detail and description they have practised *(see Chapter 7 - Stamina with Style)*.

Planning the Weekly Foci for the Suave Writing Session

The focus for the week's writing should move around the curriculum from week to week. This allows the school to count the suave writing session as time from the budget of other subjects. Thus, in the upcoming example, the half term's extended writing sessions would count as up to 50 minutes from English in week one, science in week two, history in week three, and so on.

In addition, the foci for the weekly extended writing should move around the types of text that the class has already been taught in dedicated English lessons, thus providing further opportunities to respond to a particular audience and purpose with a relevant text.

The following exemplifies how a class of nine to ten-year-olds might organise their independent writing foci for one half term. By week three, pupils of this age and older should be starting to use the suave features that are being taught in the short Talk:Write sessions and embedded through the suave writing sessions.

Exemplar Half-Term Timetable

Each suave writing session will use the up to 50 minutes required from the time budget of the listed subject.

Week	Subject	Text Type	Task
1	English	Narrative	Write in response to class story or other stimuli.
2	Science	Report	Write in response to investigation in science or another subject.
3	History	Diary	Write in response to experiences of an individual in history.
4	Geography	Letter	Write in response to concerns about an environmental issue in geography.
5	PSHCE	Persuasive	Write in response to a class concern in PSHCE.
6	English	Playscript	Write in response to class story or other English stimuli.
7	Geography	Discursive	Write in response to a climate change issue in geography.

How Long Is a Suave Writing Session?

- **4 to 7-year-olds** may 'write' for up to 10 minutes once a week. Young children may only be asked to write unsupported for 10 minutes initially, and they may have a small selection of other interesting activities available on their tables in case they tire of writing. This helps to prevent them disturbing the other children. There may be a dot-to-dot (excellent practice for pencil control), a simple word game, or an attractive picture book.

- **7 to 9-year-olds** might write unsupported for between 15 and 30 minutes. They may gradually build up to writing for 30 minutes or more at a time. They will have a similar selection of alternative choices as the youngest children, plus simple word searches or other word games for if they run out of ideas or stamina.

- **9 to 12-year-olds** should slowly increase from 30 minutes to 50 minutes. They will have crosswords, more challenging word searches, or age-appropriate reading books for if they run out of stamina.

The silence while the class writes, unsupported, is quite spiritual and children soon grow to love it and to react negatively if someone disturbs it. Within two or three weeks, all children will quietly put their writing to one side if they feel they have finished and occupy themselves silently with one of the choices in the middle of the table.

Exemplar ages are a guide only and will vary from class to class and school to school, however it is important that children's abilities are not underestimated. What they cannot do now may not reflect what they will be able to do in a very short period, such as two or three weeks.

Planning and Preparation on the Morning of the Suave Writing Session

The last 15 minutes of the lesson most immediately before the suave writing session is a Talk:Write session that starts with 5 minutes of refresher games and activities focused on new and relevant generic words for the writing that day, followed by 10 minutes of silent planning time for everyone.

Children may choose how they wish to plan. Several different ways to plan writing should be taught across the school. This might start with the normal text box approach that complements length, detail and description, for children aged six and above. Very young children may just write single words in the frames or draw simple pictures, while older children may write phrases and sentences.

Other planning formats include cartoon strips, thought clouds, flowcharts, spider diagrams, or just making numbered notes.

Setting the Scene for the Weekly Suave Writing Session

There are five features to the weekly suave writing sessions:

1. Atmosphere.
2. Silence.
3. Special materials.
4. Length through detail and description (LDD).
5. Time prompts with treats.

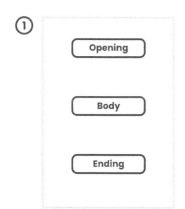

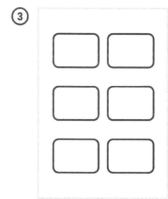

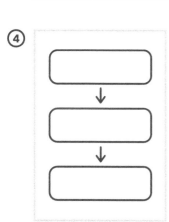

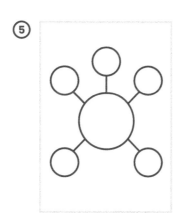

1. Atmosphere

- Create a special atmosphere in the classroom to relax children. Soften the lighting (e.g. close the blinds, turn off all or some of the lights). Remember children can cope with, and actually prefer, classroom lighting much dimmer than we normally have it.
- Put a large flickering candle up on the whiteboard to enhance the atmosphere. (Search online for meditation candle).
- Play *extremely* soft and gentle atmospheric music – the meditation candle videos usually have meditation music with them. The volume should be so low that the music cannot be heard unless the room is totally silent. Some individuals find music intrusive to thought processes, others find it complements them. Playing gentle music (instrumental only) at a volume that can scarcely be heard caters to both preferences.

2. Silence

- Expect total silence while the class are writing, save for the extremely soft music and the teacher's time prompts.

3. Special Materials

- Provide special books for the suave writing sessions – or lined paper with a margin and folders or display books.
- Provide special writing pens that are not used in other lessons.

- Place silent choices for early finishers in the centre of the blocks of tables or desks. These may be activities such as age-appropriate examples of dot-to-dot words or pictures, tracing, word searches, or reading or picture books.

4. Length Through Detail and Description

- Use the LDD structure *(see Chapter 7 – Stamina with Style)* for scaffolding the writing, enabling children to write for extended periods with stamina and style.
- Place three special treats on the tables for use in LDD for the first few weeks of suave writing sessions.

5. Time Prompts

- Use time prompts and treats to enable children to pace themselves and manage their time.

The teacher meets the class at the door and calms them as they come in. Their writing materials should be on their tables or desks already, alongside three special treats to eat. The soft music should be playing, and the lights should be dim. Adults smile and nod as the class seat themselves in silence. They may put a finger to their lips to indicate silence, if necessary. The titles for the choices should be displayed on the wall or on a flipchart and children should have been prepared on what to expect.

As soon as all are seated, the signal (which may only be a smile and a nod) should be given for them to start to write. Immediately all are engrossed, the teacher moves to one of the empty children's seats, sits, and takes up their own pen and paper, modelling themselves as a writer.

Nobody speaks...

The Role of the Adults in Suave Writing Sessions

Normally, when children are writing unsupported, many teachers move around the room making comments and suggestions. This behaviour is seen as part of the role of teaching and is often looked for in observations by many senior leaders or inspectors.

In Talk:Write, not only is the wonderful, silent, and uninterrupted experience a crucial element for the children, but it is also an important opportunity for the teacher to see exactly where the child now is in their progress towards becoming an independent suave writer. The weekly, unsupported writing is used, therefore, to track pupils' progress in the basic skills of writing, in the organisation and use of features of the type of text required, and also in the development of writer's voice.

Thus, the teacher or other adult does not intervene in the children's silent writing, although intervention and support are always provided when children write at other times of the week. They stay in their seats and model the behaviour of a writer. They may be working on their own work or actually completing a model piece of the writing task given, which they can read to the children later. The teacher only speaks to give the time prompts.

In the first two or three sessions, children may seek the help or support of the teacher, but if they always receive the same responses they will soon learn to work truly independently. The teacher should smile at them and say something like: *'It's alright Jay, I want your ideas for writing today, not more of my own. And don't be afraid of making mistakes, nobody will get anything 'wrong' in their writing today.'* Because this response is made publicly across the room, other children who might have sought the help of an adult also hear it and are more likely to work on independently. Of course, if a child looks distressed, a whispered conversation is always appropriate, or the teacher may rearrange the seating so that they sit next to the stressed child and give them support with an occasional friendly smile.

You do want the children to write without support, because you want to see where they still need help, new teaching, or a repeat of prior teaching, and you want to see if they are making progress. After the first two or three weeks, the weekly progress should be real and measurable for all children through this opportunity for formative assessment.

The Time Prompts

The closing time prompts may be given to all children by saying, *'You have X minutes left to write'; 'You have five minutes left to write'; 'You have two minutes left to finish your writing'; 'Pens down.'*

With older children who have 50 minutes altogether, the teacher may give a time prompt after 15 minutes – adjust the time as appropriate. *'You have had 15 minutes, you should be finishing your opening paragraph. Have you written about at least three of the six LDD words? Have you stopped to describe* at least one? Eat a treat and move down.' Repeat this after 30 minutes – adjust the time as appropriate. *'You have had 30 minutes, you should be finishing the main body of your work. Have you written about at least four of the LDD words? Have you stopped to describe at least three? Eat a treat and move down.'*

Repeat this after 45 minutes – adjust the time as appropriate. *'You have five minutes left to finish off your work. Have you written about at least three of the six LDD words in your ending? Have you stopped to describe at least one? Eat a treat and move down'.*

The three treats provided help to embed structure and organisation through paragraphing. They may be grapes or segments of satsumas, or even small sweets like dolly mixtures for the first few weeks, as incentives.

Written Feedback for Suave Writing Sessions

Even in the face of needing to reduce workload for teachers, the weekly suave writing should still be carefully read and commented on in writing by the teacher. There may be other writing completed in the week that is discussed with the child or reviewed orally, but with suave writing it is important to give quality feedback to every child through a short paragraph of comment that:

1. Responds positively to the child's response to the stimulus, both in the type of text and in the content e.g. *'I did enjoy your letter Safia, and you explained your worry about litter so clearly. Well done.'*

2. Celebrates one or two strengths or attempts at new skills e.g. *'Your use of a range of different suave sentence openers was very good, and I especially liked the fact that you had used alliteration in the opening.'*

3. Gives a prompt for a further area for development e.g. *'Please try to use a wider range of punctuation next week, perhaps including an exclamation mark.'*

When the writing is returned to the children, they should read your comments together in twos and discuss them. Thus, the less able readers are supported in their understanding of what you have said by working with a friend.

Embedding New Learning

When a new element of language is introduced in a ten-minute Talk:Write session, it is used repeatedly in following Talk:Write sessions and throughout other lessons across the curriculum. It is then expected that children will start to use it in their writing within a few days or weeks. When one child uses it, a great fuss and celebration takes place to encourage others to do the same. With younger children, do remind them what you would be excited to see in their writing each week.

To make a huge fuss of their successes – even though new skills may not be embedded yet – read some examples aloud glossing over grammar and punctuation errors. Celebrate – especially the unexpected child, male role models, and so on. Do not ask children to read out their own writing unless they are fluent and confident readers. If the teacher reads out the writing, they can make it sound even better than it is and verbally correct the one or two errors, thus protecting self-esteem and providing incentive to others.

Chapter 7 – Stamina with Style

Children who are developing as writers for the first time, or children who have developed negative attitudes towards writing, may find the process of writing extremely tiring. They may suffer from arm, wrist, or hand fatigue through lack of physical stamina, or from mental fatigue through a lack of sufficient language, creative thought, or processing skills. The following are some activities these children need to build stamina:

- **Learn to talk at length:** Become accustomed to talking to a group or the class, including the provision of detail and description, about things they are learning across the curriculum.

- **Learn to verbalise images in words:** Describe things in detail e.g. illustrations and pictures, videos, effects and events in electronic games, popular scenes in books and movies, amusing events in school and TV programmes, etc. Develop this into talking at length in groups and to the class.

- **Learn to create verbal visions:** Describe their own bedrooms, homes, family members, pets, favourite games, books, videos, etc. (may not be true); fictitious characters, settings, and events.

- **Learn to structure extended writing:** Through three or more paragraphs as described in the following section.

- **Rearrange furniture:** Seat the class in an open horseshoe or sit on the floor or on chairs in a circle. Discuss freely across and around the class to develop and enrich descriptions of things that might be seen, heard, smelt, tasted, felt, and so on in different settings and situations.

- **Exercise the fingers, wrists, and arms:** Encourage children to 'take a break' when writing to stretch and bend the fingers, wrist, and writing arm – and to massage gently with the other hand. Squidgy balls and other malleable aids can be an enjoyable support here.

- **Work on centre patterns and complex dot-to-dot pictures:** Use pencil or pen as brain breaks between or within lessons to strengthen grip and mobility. These can easily be found online.

- Play *describe describe describe, see page 99.*

Length Through Detail and Description (LDD) Cards

Teachers should use three A4 white cards for the key words for LDD. They should write – in large print with a thick, black marker – 'Opening' on one card, 'Body' (or 'Middle') on the second card, and 'Ending' on the third card.

Then take 18 A4 cards in three different pastel colours, and divide them into three sets of six matching cards. Again, using large print with a thick, black marker, they should write one word on each of the six cards in a set, producing three completed identical sets on three different pastel-coloured cards. These sets might be made by one or more talented members of staff for all the classes. The six different words are:

- Who?
- What?
- When?
- Where?
- Why?
- How?

A class new to this process should play games with these cards as a class.

Three children stand at the front of the classroom, each holding up one of the white cards, in the order they happen in a piece of writing. That is:

1. Opening
2. Body
3. Ending

They spread out so that the opening is on the extreme left, the body is in the middle, and the ending is on the extreme right.

The teacher then names a well-known story and calls on a child to bring a Who? card to stand by the opening card child. They must say who the person or people are in the opening of the story. Then a child carrying a Where?, What?, or When? card may be called by the teacher and, as these cards are brought out, the children holding them up cluster round the opening. Either the child carrying the card or members of the class state where the characters were or where they went, why they were there, what they were doing or were going to do, and when it all happened. They then might say how something happened and children could choose one card to stop and describe in detail e.g. one of the characters, the setting, the events, the weather, the character's feelings, or something similar.

The same process is then repeated in the middle of the room as children holding the second set of six cards cluster round the body card. Each child, or members of the class, now explain who appears in the body of the story who was not in the opening. Children name new features for the where, when, why, what, or how as appropriate, bringing the appropriate cards with them. Children then stop and describe two or more of these features in detail.

This is all then repeated for the ending, with class members describing one or more features in detail.

Note that, after a simple introductory experience, most stories require two or more of a particular card in one section of the story. For example, there may be two or more characters in the opening. There may be two or more events and three characters in the body. There may be two emotions in the ending. When a class has analysed two or three stories in this way, they might make up a story by naming class members, strange venues, events, and so on. This should be a fun activity with lots of laughter, but also with rich and varied descriptions and explanations.

Example of Introducing LDD

Little Red Riding Hood

Opening

Who? – Little Red Riding Hood
Who? 2 – Mother
What? – Going for a walk
When? – One sunny day
Where? – In the woods
Why? – To take grandma some food
How? – Happily; skipping

Body

Who? – Little Red Riding Hood
What? – Entered Grandma's bedroom
When? – After arriving at her cottage
Who? 2 – Wolf in the bed
Why? – Pretending to be Grandma
How? – Dressed in her nightie

Ending

Who? – Little Red Riding Hood
Who? 2 – Wolf
What? – Says he is going to eat her
Who? 3 – Woodcutter
What? – Runs in
Why? – To save Little Red Riding Hood
What? – He chases the wolf away
How? – Angrily

Using the LDD System

As soon as the class are familiar with the structure and elements of a piece of writing, the teacher displays the three white key cards across the top of one of the three walls visible to the seated class, with the opening card to the extreme left, the body card in the middle, and the ending card on the extreme right. A set of six pastel cards are clustered in an oval around each of the three key cards.

Time Prompts and Treats

When the children sit down to write, they find three 'treats' on their tables. The teacher talks through the following process and then implements it as the children write. This example is based on a 50-minute session. Adjust the timing for shorter sessions.

- After 10 to 15 minutes of writing, the teacher says: *'You have had X minutes, you should be completing the opening. Have you written about at least three of the pastel cards? Have you stopped to describe one or more? Eat a treat and move down.'*

- After 15 to 20 minutes of further writing, the teacher says: *'You have had X minutes, you should be completing the body of your story. Have you written about at least three of the pastel cards? Have you stopped to describe two or more? Please stretch your arms, wrists, hands and fingers. Eat a treat and move down.'*

- After 10 further minutes of writing, the teacher says: *'You have had X minutes, you should be completing the ending of your story. Have you written about at least two of the pastel cards? Have you stopped to describe one or more? Eat a treat and move down.'*

- 5 minutes before the end of the writing time, the teacher says: *'You have 5 minutes left to write. Please write the ending for your writing.'*

- At the end, the teacher says: *'Pens down, writing time is finished. Please stretch your arms and hands. Now, read through your writing and see if there are any quick changes you wish to make. Please use the insertion mark (∧) to show (above the line) what you would like to include.'*

After two extended writing sessions as described here, almost all children will be able to sustain the writing for the allowed period most weeks. The occasional child, who may not always be able to sustain, has silent choices in the middle of the table (as the younger children do) for when they run out of stamina.

The teacher may now add an extra prompt into each section, to encourage the use of suave features.

- Time prompt one insert: *'Has anyone used a suave word yet?'*

- Time prompt two insert: *'Has anyone used a suave sentence opener yet?'*

- Time prompt three insert: *'Have you all used a suave connective or a piece of suave punctuation?'*

The final 10 minutes of the hour, or the first 10 minutes after the next break, should be for proof reading and editing before the writing is given in to the teacher.

Small, wrapped sweets make excellent treats for the first few weeks of the process, to embed the good practice of paragraphing. If this is against school policy, then grapes or segments of mandarin oranges – wrapped in foil or cling film – are also helpful.

Supporting Structure

This system not only builds stamina, it also enables a three paragraph structure with detail and description in each paragraph. As the class grow in confidence, the body section may be repeated twice or three times (to relate three different stages of the development of the piece), in order to extend the length of pieces of writing. The teacher will talk to the class first, explaining a range of events that might take place in two or three sections of a piece of writing, with changes to location, arrival of new characters, or other developments in a plot or context. For non-fiction writing, the process is the same but the three sections might address the habitat, diet, and behaviours of an animal or the location, population, and famous features of a locality.

As children get used to extended writing and become comfortable with the structure, this will settle down into the standard time prompts, *(see Chapter 6 - The Suave Writing Session)*.

Chapter 8 – Progress Steps for Composition

Exemplar teaching objectives by age can be created by breaking each item into one or two specific examples.

These are approximate models for steps in sentence structure as children move from talk through to impact on writing. Pupils may reach these steps in different orders and at different stages. With younger children, it may be a few weeks before impact is seen in writing, whereas older children and/or more able children may start trying to use some of the new features almost immediately.

Talk:Write doesn't require any particular writing assessment process, however it is important that your school has a system in place. For schools without such a system, we recommend *Oxford Primary Writing Assessment* (Oxford University Press). Formative assessment is key to ensuring that a teacher knows which skills pupils do and don't possess. This feeds into planning so that the gaps are addressed.

Please note that these progress steps are not designed to be turned into a tick list or assessed against.

The evidence of impact will be seen in the children's weekly unsupported writing and in their writing across the curriculum.

A tabulated version of these progress steps is available to download from our website.

Age 4 to 5

1. Talk for all purposes in sentences of three words or more.
   - Can talk about what we did at home.
   - Can talk about our favourite TV programmes.
   - Can talk about what we like doing best in school.
2. Start oral sentences in different ways e.g. I, my, the, this, he, she, it, etc.
   - Can start sentences in different ways e.g. *'I like milk.'; 'My dog barks.'; 'She can run.'; 'The dog is brown.'*
3. Join oral sentences using simple conjunctions e.g. and, but, so, if.
   - Can use conjunctions to join two sentences e.g. *'I like milk and I like cake.'; 'I was late so I ran.'*

1. Talk in a continuous stream of simple sentences.
   - Can talk confidently for a few minutes about something they know well e.g. what they do at the weekend.
2. Extend many sentences using connectives e.g. and, but, so, if, when, because.
   - Can use more than three different connectives (need not be all at once) e.g. *'I like milk when I have my cereal, but I do not like it on its own because sometimes it tastes bad. It goes bad in the sun and if it is in a hot place.'*
3. Use simple adjectives in speech e.g. good, bad, nice, wet, dry, sunny, etc.
   - Can use adjectives in talk e.g. *'I like tea in my red mug.'; 'It is a sunny day.'; 'We played a new game.'*

1. Talk confidently, mainly in simple sentences.
   - Can talk for several minutes continuously, with confidence e.g. about a pet, a favourite story, or a television programme.
2. Use a range of simple sentence openers e.g. person – I, You, He, She, They, etc.; determiners – The, A, This, That; sequence openers – First, Next, Last, Before, After, etc.; time openers – Today, This morning, Yesterday, Next week, On Saturday, etc.
   - Can start sentences in different ways e.g. *'You are a good reader.'; 'That is a good book.'; 'After school, I play out.'; 'Yesterday, I went shopping.'*
3. Change sentence openers when asked, sometimes using time or sequence words, or adverbs.
   - Can change the sentence opener when asked e.g. *change the opener game: 'At the weekend, I went to the park.'; 'On Saturday, I went to the park.'; 'First, I went to the park.'; 'Quickly, I went to the park.'*
4. Use a wider range of simple adjectives and adverbs in oral sentences e.g. adjectives – happy, sad, old, pretty, ugly, etc.; adverbs – slowly, quickly, angrily, quietly, etc.
   - Can use a wide range of describing words (adjectives and adverbs) e.g. *'The tired dog looks sad.'; 'The old house is ugly.'; 'She ran quickly down the long road.'*
5. Use a wider range of connectives in talk e.g. and, but, so, when, if, because, too, as well as, etc.
   - Can use a wide range of connectives to join or extend sentences e.g. *'I will go to the shop, if it stops raining.'; 'I ate a bun as well as my soup.'; 'Can you play out when you get home?'*
6. Start sentences in a wider range of ways, including with adverbs, time and sequence connectives, and a wider range of connectives when asked.
   - Can start sentences in a wider range of ways including 'ly' words and connectives e.g. *'When I went to the park…'; 'If I had been to the park…'; 'After I had been to the park…'; 'Slowly, I went to the park…'*

7. Use given suave words in games and activities.

   - Can use one or two suave words in games e.g. *'Can anyone remember what hesitantly means?'; 'Can you start a sentence with hesitantly?'; 'Where could you put hesitantly in this sentence?'; 'I climbed the stairs at bedtime.'; Show two options e.g. 'I climbed the stairs hesitantly...'; 'Hesitantly, I climbed...'*

Age 7 to 8

1. Begin to open sentences in a wider range of ways in own talk e.g. time connectives, sequence connectives, adverbs ('ly' words), gerunds ('ing' words), or a wider range of connectives: when, if, because.

   - Can use 'ly' openers e.g. *'Gently, I lifted up the pretty kitten.'*
   - Can use 'ing' openers e.g. *'Hoping to be first, I raced to the shop.'*
   - Can use connective openers e.g. *'Because I was late, I missed the bus.'*

2. Start to use a wider range of suave sentence openers in games and activities (gerunds – 'ing' words).

   - E.g. suave word to open the sentence: *'Hesitantly, I opened the box.'; 'Hungrily, I devoured the sandwich.'; 'Doing exercise is good for your health.'; 'As we ate lunch, we talked about our pets.'; 'Reading is my best hobby.'; 'Watching TV makes me sleepy.'*

3. Begin to use a wider range of adjectives and adverbs in own talk.

   - Can use a range of describing words (adjectives and adverbs) e.g. *'I like sweet fruit and ice cream.'; 'Jon ran quickly to the shop.'; 'Mum always buys amazing cakes.'*

4. Use some suave connectives e.g. as, as well as, instead of, although, when prompted.

   - Can use a range of connectives e.g. *'Instead of football, we went swimming.'; 'I like hot dogs, although Mum doesn't buy me them.'*

5. Use a wider range of time and sequence connectives e.g. early on, after, soon after, shortly before, just before, after that, after a while, in a short time, etc.

   - Can use one or two suave connectives e.g. despite, contrary to, although.
   - E.g. time and sequence connectives: *'I shall go to the market tomorrow, if it doesn't rain.'; 'Just before it rained, I dashed to the store.'; 'We went for a river side walk soon after the rain stopped.'; 'Next, we had our lunch.'*

6. Name and use a wider range of punctuation in games and activities e.g. . ! ? , ' " "

   - Can recognise and name six or more pieces of punctuation e.g. *'How many different sorts of punctuation has Bud used? Name them? Where could he have used a question mark?'*

7. Use a wider range of suave words in talk and games when prompted.

1. Join in games and activities to use a wide range of suave words e.g. nouns, verbs, adjectives, adverbs, gerunds, and connectives.
   - *(see Chapter 10 - Games, Activities, and Examples).*

2. Use connectives such as although, however, despite, in spite of, unless, contrary to, nevertheless, etc. in games and activities.
   - Can use some suave connectives e.g. *'I went for a walk despite the rain.'; 'Despite being hungry, I finished my homework.'; 'Contrary to rules, I ate my sweet in the classroom.'; 'I like hot dogs, however Mum doesn't buy me them.'; 'I hurried to the bus stop, nevertheless I missed the bus.'*

3. Name and use a wide range of punctuation in games and activities e.g. . ! ? , ' ... "" ( ) –
   - Can name and use a wide range of punctuation (eight or more) e.g. *'Punctuate Bud's work for him and then say what punctuation it needed.'*

4. Talk confidently and fluently.
   - Can talk, without preparation, about recent experiences, family, pets, learning, or things they have enjoyed.

5. Change the style of talk from local speak to both Standard English and suave speak, and back, in games and activities.
   - Can change confidently between local speak, Standard English, and suave speak e.g. *'Oh dear, Bud has written in local speak today. It says, "Us went ter t' shop." Can you turn it into Standard English please?'*

6. Change the voice for questions, exclamation, suspense, anticipation, and volume.
   - Can use appropriate expression in speaking voice when reading aloud.

7. Explain features of different types of writing e.g. letter, diary item, report, explanation.
   - Can name the features of three or more types of writing.

1. Talk confidently and fluently in a range of situations e.g. chat, role play, discussion, presentation, debate.
   - Can change the tone and type of talk easily for different purposes.
   - Can use a range of suave connectives.
   - Can use a range of different and interesting sentence openers.

2. Change the style and tone of speech appropriately for context and purpose.
   - Can use the different codes of speech in writing as appropriate.
   - Can make characters sound cross, surprised, excited, etc.

3. Use a range of different types of connectives in talk e.g. although, however, despite, contrary to, unless, nevertheless, additionally, in addition, furthermore, except, alternatively, consequently, including, etc. in games and activities.
   - Can use suave connectives e.g. *'Which is the connective in this sentence?'; 'Spot the connectives.'; 'Suave up the connective in this sentence.'; 'Insert suave connectives in the spaces.'*

4. Open sentences in a range of different ways with confidence, when talking: time, sequence, adverbs ('ly' words), connectives, gerunds ('ing' words) e.g. *'Hoping to see…'; 'Rushing down the road, I…'; 'Carrying the heavy…'*

   - Can use suave sentence openers e.g. *'Can you put a suave opener at the beginning of each of these sentences?'; 'Can you underline the suave sentence openers in Bud's writing?'; 'Can you change two of the sentence openers in Bud's work to suave openers?'*

5. Start to use literary features in oral games and activities e.g. groupings, clauses, dialect, metaphor, simile, alliteration, onomatopoeia.

   - Can use one or more literary features in writing and games.

   - Can use one or more literary features e.g. *'Bud has written in local speak again. Please turn it into suave speak with a literary feature.'; 'Where has Bud used a literary feature today?'; 'Spot the literary features in this passage.'*

   - Starting to use literary features e.g. grouping: *'The small red box, the shabby old book, and the tube of sweets all fell out of my bag.'*; clauses: *'The scared little dog, left alone by the path, waited for his owner to come.'*; dialect: *'The old woman looked up as I passed and grumbled, "Yer bes' not ride yer bike on't grass yer knows."'*; metaphor: *'He has a heart of gold.'*; simile: *'He is as old as the hills.'*; alliteration: *'The cute and cuddly cat curled up on the cushion.'*; onomatopoeia: *'The hiss of the snake…'*

6. Change the voice or language to model different types of punctuation e.g. exclamation, question, parenthesis (asides and embedded clauses), quotation within speech.

   - Can use a variety of punctuation for different effects in writing and change the voice appropriately when reading the writing aloud e.g. exclamations: *'The man shouted, "Get out!"'*; questions: *'The man sighed, "Will I ever get home?"'*; parenthesis: *'Mrs Green, head of the school, made me very welcome.', 'Bats – often seen at dusk – are nocturnal creatures.', 'Ellie took my last sweet (she was always doing that) and ate it!'*; quotation within speech: *'The teacher began, "I want you all to think of a famous quotation you know, such as 'Beware the Ides of March,' and find a reason to use it in your writing today."'*

7. Explain the characteristics of most genres / types of text.

8. Change the register of speech for different purposes e.g. Standard English, received pronunciation, or suave speak; local speak or dialect.

Age 10 to 11

1. Use all the strategies for 9 to 10-year-olds with confidence.
2. Talk fluently and confidently, most of the time.
3. Change the voice, register, or accent for different purposes.
4. Structure sentences in a wide range of different ways for interest.
5. Use a wide range of literary features in games and activities to model understanding and fluency.
6. Start to use a range of sophisticated features such as the passive voice, complex groupings, or implicit links / references forwards and backwards between paragraphs and sections in games and activities.
   - Can use a range of literary features and techniques e.g. passive voice: *'The cake was eaten by the child.'*; complex grouping: *'All their favourite foods were there: chicken legs with curried rice; fat sausages with golden chips; cheesecake covered in ice cream; and the biggest slices of birthday cake you could wish for.'*; implicit link back: *'It all ended well and Jo's early fear that his mother might not get back safely was proved to be totally wrong.'*
7. Can present at length, orally, on one subject.

Age 11 Plus

1. Able to do all of the above for 10 to 11-year-olds through planned activities.
2. Demonstrate differences between local speak, Standard English, and suave speak with confidence and fluency.
3. Adjust tone, expression, and register for need.
4. Take part in public discussions, debates, and performances.
5. Use a wide range of suave speak, adjusted for purpose and audience.
6. Use a wide range of literary features in games and activities to show understanding.
7. Know, understand, and spell all words in the tier 2 lists.
8. Know and understand many tier 3 words.
9. Check back on all the recommendations and examples for previous age groups. Can your class use them all when appropriate?

A list of tier 2 and 3 words can be downloaded from our website.

Model Extracts for the Progress Steps

Schools should institute regular review points into the academic year. Once a term or twice a year, teachers should be assessing each child's progress since the last review point. They should compare copies of the child's independent writing from the previous review point with their latest unsupported writing, and the progress should be visible. This will be better facilitated if the subject of the writing is similar or the same as at the previous review point. It should also be possible to identify improvements in basic skills, if needed, and new or more developed suave features in language, increased confidence, and ability to express ideas.

It is good practice for teachers to copy every child's final piece of assessed writing for the year and insert it into the child's records. In the case of unsupported, extended writing, a display album or slim ring binder is ideal for storage of this writing. Thus, parents, managers, and other involved people can easily analyse a child's progress in writing from one year to the next.

The following examples take the teacher through the development of sentence structure, illustrating the progress commonly expected by the end of each academic year.

The writing exercise book or portfolio should go forward to the receiving teacher when the class moves, and the teacher should ensure that all children are quickly back to writing at their standard from the end of the previous year. Some children regress over the long summer break as they do little or no writing in the holiday. For some children with EAL, their English may also regress if they are living and playing in homes and a community where English is rarely in use.

It is important to recognise that the age range is only a guide, that summer born children are up to a year younger than their peers, and that some younger children may be more able.

There are supporting comments and explanations in the right hand column of the examples to indicate significant areas of progress.

Mark Making

Pre-School

I have a mum. I have a dad. my dad is big.

From mark making to simple words and –
for some – simple sentences.

Age 5 to 6

I have a mum and a dad. My dad is big. I have
a sista two.

Joins two simple sentences with
first connectives.

Uses adverb 'too' (although incorrectly spelt)
to mean also or as well.

Spelling mistake.

Age 6 to 7

I have a mum and a dad. My dad is big and
my mum werks in school. I have a sister too.
Me and my sister go to school and my dad
drives a big truck. It has eight weels and it is
red and gold. My dad took me for a ride in his
truck. It was fun.

Up to one side of A4.

Adds information for interest.

Uses two descriptive clauses joined by
a connective.

Spelling mistakes.

Age 7 to 8

In my family I have a mum and a dad and a sister. I also have two dogs. One of our dogs is big and one of them is small. We live in one of the flats behind the school. We live on floor 7 and when the lift is broke we have to clime all the stairs. I dont like it when we have to clime the stares.

Up to one side of A4.

Opens sentence with a clause for context.

Uses connective 'also' to create a link to the previous sentence.

Uses preposition 'behind' to create adjectival phrase for which flats.

Uses 'when' as a time connective.

Expresses opinion.

Noun/verb mismatch (the lift is broken).

Apostrophe for contraction is missing.

Spelling mistakes.

Age 8 to 9

My family live in Westborne Court, which is behind the school. It is a huge block of flats and we live on the seventh floor. Although it can be noisy and a bit smelly in the stairwell, I like living there because I have a lot of friends and we play on the grass between our flats and Marlboro Court. We have 2 dogs and my dad takes them for a walk every morning. My mum usually takes them after school. She is a teaching asistant in Year 3. When my dad has to bring his enormous truck home all our neihbors grumble because there isn't enough room for their cars.

Up to one and a half sides of A4.

Correctly uses a comma.

Uses 'which' as a pronoun to create a link for extension into a phrase for location.

Uses suave word 'huge'.

Uses suave sentence opener 'although'.

Correctly uses comma after opening clause.

Uses connective 'because' to give a reason.

Uses adverb of time 'usually'.

Uses preposition 'after' as a time connective to say when something happens.

Opens sentence with time connective 'when'.

Uses suave word 'enormous'.

Correctly uses apostrophe for contraction.

Spelling mistakes.

Westborne Court is a twelve-story block of apartments behind our school. My family have lived here for all my life, in fact my mum says I was nearly born in the lift! I am the oldest of two children. My sister, Daisy, is two years younger than me. Despite the lift breaking regularly, we all love living here. There are two large bedrooms, a lounge, a kitchen and a bathroom. Outside our flats there is a large area of grass with a road running all the way round it. We play football and chasing on the grass, and there are two benches where we often sit and chat. Although I have lots of friends in this block of flats, my best friend lives in Marlborough Court on the other side of the grass. His name is Jamie and he is in my class at school. Sometimes Jamie and I go down the hill to play on the school playing fields at the weekends.

Up to two sides of A4.

Correctly uses a comma.

Uses humour and exclamation mark.

Correctly uses double commas for parenthesis.

Uses preposition connective 'despite' to open a sentence. This is a suave sentence opener.

Uses simple grouping with a list with one or more items being qualified with adjectives.

Uses location preposition 'outside' to open a sentence. This is a suave sentence opener.

Uses preposition 'with' as a connective.

The sentence needs to be read aloud and checked for grammar and punctuation.

Have you ever visited Westborne Court? I think you would have a pleasant surprise if you did. It is not how many people think it is – we don't have any dealers or gangs here – although my friend, Jamie, says they do in Marlborough Court across The Green. Westborne Court has been my home for my entire life. My mum says that she always wanted to live here and when she and my dad got married, they were so excited to get this apartment. I love the lounge, it is quite big and has expansive windows that look across to Marlborough Court.

My sister and I share a bedroom at the back by the kitchen (I wish we didn't have to share) and sometimes people wake me in the night by banging on the windows when they are walking along the passage to their homes. Mum and Dad are both talking about us relocating to a proper house with three bedrooms so that Daisy and I can have our own rooms. Also, now Dad has lost his job as a truck driver because the company went bust, he says he would like a garden to grow some vegetables. Despite all the disadvantages of living here, I really do love it and don't want to relocate anywhere else.

Up to two sides of A4, or sometimes more.

Correctly uses question mark for a sophisticated opening using a rhetorical question.

Uses suave word adjective 'pleasant'.

Correctly uses double dashes for parenthesis.

Correctly uses double commas for parenthesis.

Uses expanded noun phrase including suave word.

Uses adverb 'always' to qualify statement.

Uses adverb 'quite' as qualifier.

Uses suave word 'expansive'.

Uses paragraphs.

Correctly uses brackets for parenthesis.

Uses suave word 'relocating'.

Uses suave sentence opener including preposition as connective.

Uses suave sentence opener 'despite'.

Correctly uses apostrophe for contraction.

There are definitely pros and cons to living in Westborne Court on the Topmoor Estate; I will discuss a few of them with you now. This block of apartments in the north of the city has been my home since my birth in 2009, and I am extremely happy living here. Our apartment – which is on the seventh floor of twelve – is exceptionally cosy with bright, warm rooms and a splendid view from the lounge past Marlborough Court (where my best friend lives) and out over the heart of the city. Despite the fact that I share a bedroom with my sister (still!) we manage very well and Mum bought a screen so that we have some privacy between our halves of the room.

As a family, we get on well with all our neighbours and my parents seem to be well liked due to the fact that they will always help others if they are in trouble. My mum still takes a meal to the old man, George, in the adjacent apartment to us every evening. I tend not to play on The Green anymore, that is mainly for kids, but I do meet my friends at the bus shelter and we enjoy a good laugh. Some of them smoke a cigarette, but I never do because my granddad died from smoking.

The main trouble with the Topmoor Estate is that there is a gang of lads – mainly from The Terraces and a few from Marlborough Court – who hang around the playing fields by the primary school. They are called the Topmoor Gang and usually they're OK, but sometimes they just turn nasty and can attack kids passing by and steal their phones or money. Generally, I stay away from them and mind my own business. Occasionally, at the weekends, we hear sirens from police cars racing to the school and later we hear what the gang have been doing.

This may not be the most impressive place to live but, on the whole, I have enjoyed it here. Now, though, I am ready to move and am hoping that my parents are successful in getting a proper house soon; then the next phase of my life can begin!

Often over two pages.

Uses suave words 'pros and cons'.

Uses suave word 'discuss'.

Uses double dashes for embedded clause.

Uses suave word 'exceptionally'.

Uses brackets (parenthesis) for an aside.

Uses a suave sentence opener.

Uses brackets informally and exclamation mark for humorous aside.

Uses prepositional phrase as suave sentence opener.

Uses sophisticated prepositional phrase.

Uses suave connective 'due to'.

Uses suave word 'adjacent'.

Uses sophisticated verb form.

Uses sophisticated verb form.

Correctly uses double dashes for parenthesis.

Uses 'generally' as suave sentence opener.

Uses 'occasionally' as suave sentence opener.

Uses suave word 'impressive'.

Correctly uses double commas for parenthesis.

Correctly uses semi-colon.

Uses suave word 'phase'.

Missing comma to close parenthesis.

Chapter 9 – Working with Children New to English

This chapter is to support teachers in one of two scenarios. The first is teaching one or a small number of children new to English in a class where all other children are confident, first language English speakers. The second is teaching a class in English where all or almost all children are new to English. This is regardless of whether the school is implementing the Talk:Write programme in full, partially, or not at all, although the programme will certainly help these pupils as they start to build their communication skills in English. This section provides guidance and support for educators across the spectrum of bi and multilingual settings – and at the same time it includes many well-researched and common-sense ideas, approaches, and techniques for all who ever find themselves teaching in unfamiliar settings.

The whole issue of pupil talk in classrooms needs to be a priority discussion in schools and best policy and practice should be observed by all. Pupils from age 5 to 12 or more should be pro-actively encouraged to talk in almost all lessons. There are, however, a small number of lessons where silence is an asset for most pupils. These may include extended writing, silent reading, or the completion of an exercise that is to provide accurate formative or summative information. In the majority of lessons, pupils should be expected to discuss their ideas, understanding, and interpretation of activities, but they should also be totally aware that this does not include talking over the teacher or telling each other answers.

Talk within lessons must be seen as a learning tool and – at the same time – as an opportunity for further practising and embedding children's emergent Standard English if their home language features a strong local accent, dialect, patois, or street talk – or is in a language other than English.

Schools within the English speaking system report that they are increasingly receiving children who speak little or no English at point of entry; there are no actual statistics available currently. At the same time – new English speaking schools are opening in increasing numbers around the world, according to the main international providers.

Teachers are members of a deeply committed and caring profession whose primary aspiration is to see their pupils thrive, learn, and succeed. Being faced with one child or a whole class who do not understand the language the teacher is functioning in and who are unable to respond to the teaching or even to express their lack of understanding, can be an extremely stressful scenario for all involved. For many teachers, there is little or no induction or professional development to support them in this scenario. Indeed, there are many new schools opening with children new to English and existing schools where the profile of the intake is changing and where the head and senior leaders may have no prior experience of working with children new to English.

A Small Number of Pupils New to English

This situation should cause the teacher no anxiety. The curriculum should be addressed in the same way as any other new teaching would be. In fact, Talk:Write will speed the acquisition of English for the child or children new to English through increasing both the amount and the quality of talk in the classroom. When a new pupil is admitted to the school who is unable to speak or understand English as yet, the following steps should be implemented:

- Find out as much as possible about the child's prior schooling, the languages the child already does speak and understand, and any pertinent information about the circumstances of life immediately prior to their arrival in your school, such as trauma or deprivation. This may be done through the parents, community leaders, or community members who may share a common language with the new child and their parents, or through bringing in a person able to interpret and communicate with the parents and child, for a discussion on their child's needs, prior education, and other relevant information to ensure a successful and stress-free induction. The questions that would most help teachers to induct and support the new child should be carefully planned prior to the interview and should be sensitive to the cultural norms of the family.

- If possible, identify other pupils or adults within the school who speak the same language as the new pupil's first (home or original) language or who share the pupil's second or other languages. Establish access for support and discussion daily (at playtime, lunchtime, during assembly, or at another suitable time).

- If a member of the support staff in the school shares the same language as the child, that person should ideally be moved into the child's class and seated next to the child – at least for part of the day and for the first half term. This person should be briefed on what has been taught, is being taught, and is about to be taught in order for them to translate for the child.

- Place the new pupil in a class where another pupil shares their first language or where they both share a language they are competent in. Many children new to English are already bilingual or multilingual, they just do not speak English yet. If possible, seat the pupil next to the child who speaks the same language or who has another language in common. This may only be temporary if it causes the established pupil concern with regard to friendships, but most pupils are pleased to support an incoming child with whom they share a language.

- If seating a new pupil with a pupil with a shared language is not an option, seat the pupil next to someone who is a confident talker in English and is friendly, patient, and helpful.

- Explain to the supporting pupil and other children in the class that they should talk with the newly-arrived pupil in first language (if able) throughout lessons and between lessons, especially when there is learning or an activity to be explained – and in response to the child's questions.

- Explain to a supporting child who does not share a language with the new pupil that they should demonstrate and illustrate as much of the teacher's instructions as they are able to, and encourage the new pupil by making them feel welcome, included, and a part of the class.

- Always talk slowly and clearly when teaching. Make eye contact and smile while talking and touch the child on the back of the shoulder or arm at least once in every silent session, as you pass round the room, to help them feel included.

- Explain the strategies you are using to enhance access to learning for the newly-arrived pupil to the class. These should include the use of picture clues, modelling, mime, demonstration, etc. constantly interwoven to support understanding.

- Encourage pupils to talk together, to explain, to mime, and to demonstrate learning to one another constantly, replicating the teacher's techniques and trying out ideas of their own.

- Be patient and allow the child time to settle, to relax, and to start to 'tune in' to the language and the rhythms of the class.

- Teach the class short jingles, verses, and choruses that can be sung or recited within and between lessons. Rhythms and rhymes are very good hooks for new learning. Childhood songs like *Head and Shoulders – Heels and Toes*, *Ten Green Bottles*, *There Were Ten in a Bed*, *The Wheels on the Bus*, and especially *The Alphabet Song* are also very good vehicles for the teaching of relevant, key vocabulary. They should be done with the appropriate actions.

- Find songs, stories, and information from the pupils' home country and share these with the whole class.
- Start new sessions by each child saying their name loudly, slowly, and clearly.

Children of all abilities will benefit from this, not just the children new to English. Sitting in a strange classroom surrounded by children and adults who are all talking in a language you have no understanding of is extremely unsettling and very stressful for some. Patience, kindness, and calm encouragement through body language and facial expressions are crucial.

In the main, there are two quite distinct initial responses to the scenario. Some pupils will immediately start to 'try-out' occasional words and phrases they hear. Inevitably, they will get some of these wrong at first, mispronouncing them or using them in the wrong contexts. They will get sentence and phrase constructions muddled and may apply grammatical rules from home language in their emerging efforts. Such slips must never appear to be criticised. The pupil should be encouraged and praised by a small clap or a thumbs-up (a widely used sign of approval) and the actual word or phrase should be repeated for them, slowly and clearly.

Other pupils will sit in total silence for a long time after arriving in the new classroom. This could be as a reaction to the environment or language, as a result of previous disruption or trauma, or because their previous experiences of school had required that behaviour. Gradually, these children will also start to attempt communication by simple words or phrases in English. However, there are 'silent' pupils who may not speak for many weeks, months or even – in occasional cases – a few years. These children might be misunderstood – being seen as having additional needs in some way – perhaps with hearing or speech difficulties. A brief and positive discussion with parents could soon allay these fears. Almost always this is not the case – most parents would ensure the school knew of such a scenario at the time of admission. Almost always this pupil is opting to deploy the silent period while they absorb English and build their vocabulary and understanding. Then, eventually, they speak, and it will immediately be in almost totally accurate sentences that are relevant and comprehensible. Pupils passing through this silent period have been known to remain silent with teachers in the classroom for as long as up to five years, rather than risk making errors in their communications in English.

The hardest way to learn a new language is by being in a predominantly silent classroom. The newly arrived child needs to be surrounded by talk and when that talk is addressed to a group or the whole class it should generally be clear, quite loud, and quite slow. The language should be simplified – as uncluttered as possible – at least for main inputs and instruction. The teacher and support staff should observe the following examples of best practice whenever possible.

Teaching with Key Words

Key words are a crucial part of teaching for pupils new to English.

1. Key words may be nouns or verbs that are central to the aspect of teaching and the subject it is within, and they should be the simplest examples available. Thus, if learning about the life cycle of a frog, key words would probably be frog, pond, frog spawn, tadpole, and legs. All of these can and should be illustrated through diagrams and all are simple, single-syllable words – with the exception of frog spawn (but the first word will already be known through the introduction) and tadpole which can be iterated as two simple distinctive parts. If teaching about the Victorian homes, however, the essential language is much broader and there are often many choices for what might be considered essential vocabulary. On the whole, teachers should choose things that can be illustrated or mimed. These might include Queen Victoria herself, a Victorian house with the key word 'home', a framed picture with the word 'picture', some vases with the word 'vases', plates with the key word 'plates', and then furniture that will be useful for the child in school as well as in the historical learning, such as 'table', 'chair', and 'cupboard'.

2. Once the decision has been made as to which the key word will be, the teacher must stick to the use of the same word throughout oral teaching and – when members of the class use other words – should agree with them but then repeat the new word and the original key word for the benefit of the child who is new to English. For example, if the teacher chooses rug as a key word, but another child offers mat or carpet in an answer, the teacher should say something like, *'Well done, Imran, it is a mat, a rug, in front of the fire.'*

3. Key words with an illustration should be clearly displayed within view of the new child and the teacher should point to the images when talking about them. This practice enables the teacher to prepare simple tasks for the child while the rest of the class work, which could include drawing and labelling the items in the illustrations of key words,

finding examples of them in pictures and labelling them, and matching key words to the appropriate illustration when they are not immediately next to each other or are on separate cards.

4. Encourage the child who is new to English and their supporting partner to talk constantly when teaching has taken place. For the first few days, the teacher should join them as soon as possible and model going back over the key points using key words, pictures, and mime. This will also help the supporting child to develop techniques for better helping their new peer. The teacher should ensure the new child understands what the task specially prepared for them is, demonstrate what to do, and watch them start to ensure they understood. If they cannot prioritise this, they should have explained it to the supporting child.

5. If there is someone in the school (but not in this class) who shares the same first or second language as the new child, they should be asked to spend 10 to 15 minutes with the child talking them through the main points that the teacher will be making and reading the key words with them. This might be done in one playtime, part of a lunchtime, or part of an assembly.

6. At the start of a new focus of learning, the teacher or support staff should find the correct first language name for the key words in the topic through a safe, school-approved internet translation site. Support from a speaker of first language would still be needed here as interpretations can vary widely. These words, once agreed, could be included on a poster illustrating the key words and their images. They may be written two ways – the way they would normally be written in first language plus in phonetic English – so that the teacher and other class members can learn the key words in first language and use them. Adults can check they have found the right sounding word by tapping the object or illustration, for example the tabletop, and asking the child by gesture what they would call it, or by contacting a speaker of the first language to confirm it.

7. All important objects in the classroom and parts of the classroom itself – such as the door and the windows – should be clearly labelled with the simplest name for them in English and a translation into first language if possible. This should also include a phonetic version of the first language so that the teacher and others may say its name in first language when referring to it, and a small picture if there could be ambiguity as to what the word refers to.

8. When talking with the new child, try not to change the words used because the child does not understand them first time, and definitely do not repeat them at greater volume – unless you have realised you had not spoken loudly and clearly enough the first time. The child's hearing is not the barrier (unless there actually is a hearing issue for the child) – it is the new language that is the barrier. Instead, try to think of new and better ways to mime, demonstrate, illustrate, and so on or use the internet to attempt a translation. If the word sought is urgent, for example it could affect health and safety, consult the identified support within school or the parent or community leader. If it is not vital, leave it and return to it another day.

The following section is for classrooms where most children are new to English. However, it also includes many useful items for all teachers.

Most or All Pupils New to English

The previous section is written to support teachers who receive an occasional child into their class who is not yet able to speak or understand English. Some of the content will still be of interest to all teachers and may be supportive for teachers in classes where all or almost all pupils are new to English.

Ideally, when staffing a newly opening school that will function in English as the language of the classroom, efforts should be made to recruit bi or multilingual support staff for the opening term at least. Each class should have at least one support teacher who shares first language (the home or original language of the majority of the children) with the children. Many children from countries in the Middle East and the Far East are, in fact, multilingual, having two or more languages they already understand. If support staff are recruited from the families these children come from, it is likely that these members of staff will also be multilingual and thus able to support more than one group of children. The main incoming languages of the class or school should have been identified prior to recruitment and the appointments should reflect this.

Multilingual support staff should be as directly involved in the teaching as is feasible. In the early weeks, they should work at the front of the classroom with the teacher and should be translating key elements of the learning – pre-identified and agreed with the teacher – into the dominant language/s of

the classroom. When instructions are needed for a task, the support teacher should re-explain and demonstrate in first language. When children are working, the support teacher should move round re-explaining and answering questions. If they identify that there is not enough understanding generally across the class, they should notify the teacher, and all should then be re-explained in first language.

Immersion Policy or No Immersion Policy in a Newly Opened School

Immersion Policy is a whole-school policy, often rigorously implemented, that demands that no language other than English should be spoken in a school. When parents send their children to an English speaking school, it is usually because they want the child or children to become fluent speakers of English. Speaking English can be seen as enhancing a person's future career opportunities as it has become the most widely spoken language in the world. This does not mean that English is any better than any other language, and all languages should be treated with equal respect. At induction, parents should be brought together for a full explanation of how the school is organised, how it will function, the curriculum, the teaching staff, the support staff, timetabling, homework, lunchtime, and so forth. This induction should be multilingual, with translation into pre-agreed dominant languages, unless it is beyond question that all parents speak English.

Included in this induction should be information about the promotion of talk and discussion in first language as well as emerging English in the early days. Parents need to understand that, when their children are able to discuss their embryonic understanding of the taught input and instructions with their friends in first language, their shared interpretation enhances understanding for all.

Sadly, there are some teachers who fear that if children are talking in first language they are either cheating or off-task. This is very rarely the case, and it is no harder to tell whether a pair or group are discussing the work in hand or are gossiping about a TV programme when they are speaking in another language, than it is when they are speaking English. The teacher may not be able to hear what they are saying, but is almost always able to tell whether or not they are still working.

Teachers in settings where most or all of the children do not speak English should consider how they would feel if, while in a foreign country where they could not speak the language, they were suddenly required to learn that language or a life skill in that language, taught by a first language speaker who spoke no English. When the lesson starts and the teacher is talking at length in a language that the visitor does not understand, while gesturing and indicating materials or displays, the visitor would naturally wish to turn to their friend or neighbour and say things like, *'What do you think they mean?'*, *'What do you suppose we are to do?'*, *'Did you understand that?'*, and so on. Through a pooling of ideas, the recollection by some of words that are similar to words they know in other languages and the interpretation of the teacher's gestures and performance, the group may reach a common understanding that a single member might not have reached – at least of some of the teaching.

If the teacher and the rest of the class discovered that one of their number could actually understand the teacher, they would all want to ask this group member what

the teacher had said and what was to be done. This pupil could be a great asset to the teacher and to the other children's learning and understanding.

Thus, in a class where all pupils are new to English, children must be encouraged to discuss their understanding or interpretation of what the teacher has said or wants them to do and, if any child in the class understands some English or can actually speak English, the teacher who has no bilingual support should make use of this child's abilities – pro-actively asking the child to explain something to the class.

Guidance

- If there are several children with one first language in common, they should be seated together in a group to facilitate discussion.
- If there are several children who speak and understand English fluently or who are first language English speakers, they should be allocated to different groups of children who do not yet understand English.
- If there are two or more children for whom English is their first language and they do not speak the dominant first language/s of the class, these children should not be separated into non-English speaking groups except for very short periods for demonstration purposes. Very often in overseas English speaking schools there will be the children of some of the teachers and they may not be bi or multilingual.
- Keep all input and instructions brief and clear. Focus on the priorities for early learning – key words for basic skills, simple repeated phrases, and demonstration, mime, or illustrations.

- Identify the key words for new areas of learning. These may be nouns or verbs. Once a key word is identified, do not use an alternative word until all children have grasped the initial choice.

- Make cards or posters with clear and simple pictures or diagrams of the key words for learning, with the key word below in both English and the other dominant first language/s. The first language/s should be written in the form they would be written in the home country, but also in phonetic English, so that the teacher and others can use the word when indicating the object or illustration. Key words should, as far as possible, always be said in dual language. Children in the class will help with pronunciation if the teacher struggles. If they hold up scissors and say scissors in English and then 'sizez' for Urdu speakers, the pronunciation of sizez should be checked with a speaker of Urdu.

- The teacher should identify a confident child who speaks the dominant first language and 'train' them as their translator. Point to the scissors and point to themself and say, 'scissors' clearly, pointing back to the scissors. Repeat this twice. Then they should point to the child and to the scissors, with questioning body and facial language. This should be repeated until the child (or another child) offers the correct word.

- Use key word translations on visual aids, the whiteboard, and even in the teacher's own input. These are available on the internet but can also be resourced through bilingual support staff, community leaders, or parents.

Key Words

There are two main types of key words. They are:

- Generic words that apply in most or all subjects in the curriculum and / or in daily life around school. All teachers should endeavour to use the same ones for the same scenarios in the first few weeks of a new school, coupling their use with translation into home language, if possible. If the school is able, one informed member of staff or associate of the school should make flashcards for every class in the school with the key words for daily life in school on the cards in dual language. Teachers could learn the main key words in first language/s to support their pupils better. These words should be used as often as possible, with the intention that all pupils should know them within the first half term.

- Subject specific or technical words that are often specific to one subject or a group of subjects. Subject specialist teachers should be provided with these key words and be advised to use the same words and not a range of words for the same thing, as frequently as possible in teaching – as will the class teachers.

The teaching of key words is a priority in the early weeks of the new school, and all teachers have a responsibility to ensure that all or almost all pupils become confident in their understanding and use as soon as possible.

The Curriculum

School leaders should plan a curriculum that is relevant for the pupils new to English in the school. If the school is newly opening and is overseas, the curriculum should initially be embedded in the locality and history of the school's immediate community, the wider locality, and then the entire host country.

Thus, there will be much that is familiar in content for the children being taught – for the first time – in English. This will also enable widespread field study and visits to encourage the application of English through first-hand experience. As the children's understanding of English broadens, so may the scope of the curriculum.

The curriculum for pupils new to English, in their first weeks of learning, should focus strongly on the teaching of facts and language that will be most useful to them in their daily life in this new – and for many – formidable situation. Thus, children should be learning about:

- Their classroom, the names of people, and objects.
- Their school building: exploring, mapping routes, naming facilities, and so forth.
- The grounds of the school: car parks, driveways, safety, play areas, sports facilities, gardens, and so forth.
- Key staff in the school and their roles: the head, senior staff, teachers and support staff who will be involved with them, lunch staff, playground supervisors, the nurse, and so forth.
- Where to go for important reasons: parental collection points, the toilets, showers, office, sick bay, lunch hall, and so forth.
- Other buildings on the campus, if relevant: walk routes, make maps, identify where siblings are if relevant, and so forth.
- Any other important information needed for daily routines and safety.
- Names of all adults who come to their classroom regularly.
- Names for daily use of all class members.
- The alphabet taught in chunks.
- Numbers to 1,000 taught in chunks.
- Key words for: daily routines, parts of the campus they will need to visit or use, the days of the week, the months of the year, the weather, how they feel and their emotions, facial expressions, items of clothing, main external body parts, and so on.

Class teachers rarely have much influence on the over-all curriculum, however they have a crucial role in the planning of its delivery in the classroom. For the first weeks with pupils new to English, the priority is not the content of the curriculum (other than the list above), but rather the establishment of basic communication in English and the codes and practices important for all future learning. All the above should be taught in small steps with patient repetition and revisits.

Name Cards

Every pupil in a class where some or all children are new to English should have their own name card. These should be pre-made by support staff or a volunteer parent. They consist of one sheet of A4 white card folded in half so that it stands horizontally on the front of the table where each child sits. The child's first name as identified for use in school – in collaboration with the parents or guardians – is written neatly in thick, black marker, in large print and in phonetic English on both sides of the card. The name may be repeated in small writing below in the form it would be in first language. The remainder of the front and the back of the card is filled with interlocking patterns in the thick, black felt tip, similar to those seen in colouring books. The complexity of the patterns is adjusted for age.

This card will stand in front of the child at all times in lessons, to enable the child to copy their English form of their name onto any work they produce and to enable the teacher and others to learn names quickly and to use names in teaching whilst they are learning them.

The owner of the card will colour the patterns over the first week or more as part of brain breaks.

Classroom Atmosphere and Organisation

The classroom should be a warm and welcoming place with colourful displays that are mainly pictorial with key words in bold writing, both in English and in the predominant first language/s of the class.

First displays should include pictorial representations (with key word labels) of all the furnishings and teaching and learning tools the children will normally use in the classroom. These will enable teachers to point to an illustration when referring to it and pupils to go to an illustration and point to it if they are not confident enough to attempt it in English. Alternatively, they can say the name of the object out loud in first language while pointing to it, enabling the teacher to translate into English.

Pupils should be allowed to examine and discuss all these illustrations in the first days in the class. The illustrations might include:

- the door/s,
- windows,
- shelves,
- cupboards,
- bookshelves,
- chairs,
- tables or desks,
- teacher's desk,
- books,
- exercise books,
- pencils,
- pens,
- crayons,
- rubbers,
- rulers,
- paint,
- water,
- hand washing facilities, and so forth.

In addition, the actual furnishings and features of the room should all be labelled in exactly the same way as their illustrations are. The welcoming atmosphere in the classroom is highly important and is very much dependent on the demeanour of the teacher and other adults present, as well as the neat, labelled appearance of everything within it.

The teacher should:

- Be calm at all times.
- Stand still almost all the time while instructing, to prevent distractions.
- Smile.
- Make eye contact with children (unless this is culturally inappropriate in the host country).
- Touch each child appropriately on the back of the upper shoulder occasionally, when moving round the room.
- Sit beside the child for individual explanations whenever possible, rather than standing above them.
- Ensure lessons are mainly calm and peaceful.
- Ensure their voice is clear and easy to hear, but not harsh.
- Ensure teaching is 'clumped' or broken into segments of about 10 minutes (explained later).
- Provide brain breaks every 10 to 15 minutes (explained later).
- Ensure teaching is supported by regular translation if a member of staff who speaks the dominant first language/s is available.
- Ensure essential learning is repeated and repeated and repeated.
- Ensure teaching is cyclical: everything important comes back again and again.
- Ensure teaching includes miming, demonstration, illustration, flashcards, video clips, models, etc.
- Ensure teaching includes rhymes and verses, songs and singing, chanting and marching, actions, games and physical activity (explained later).

Teaching Should Be 'Clumped' into Short Blocks

It is extremely difficult for anyone of any age to concentrate for periods of more than 10 to 15 minutes on talk-driven activity delivered in a language they do not understand. Concentration is aided if visuals are in use as clues while the teacher is talking, or if they mime and demonstrate content.

Taught input should be clumped into short blocks with children given something totally different to do as short breaks throughout. These short breaks are called brain breaks in many schools, and are regarded as good practice with young children. For pupils learning in English for the first time – these are essential.

The types of activities that teachers might plan as brain breaks might only last two or three minutes or might be a related activity in their own right, such as a diagram or picture to copy or colour or to label by copying the names of parts from the whiteboard.

Examples of Brain Breaks

- A simple rhyming verse (could relate to the children's new class or school) learnt at the start of the term and repeated as needed. It should include gesture or movement. For example, this may be as simple as:

Our school is the best,
Hands and feet above the rest! (wave hands then stamp feet as named)
We all love our SCHOOL! (shouted)
(Repeat)

- A simple song related to studies, learnt at the start of the term. Examples include *Head and Shoulders – Heels and Toes*; *The Alphabet Song*; *1, 2, 3, 4, 5, Once I Caught a Fish Alive*; *Ten Green Bottles*; *The Wheels on the Bus*; *There Were Ten in a Bed*; etc. All should be accompanied by gesture or 'finger drawing'.

- Name tag: the teacher touches a child on the top of the head and all have to shout the child's name. The shouting is part of the release of pressure and increases fun.

- Name tag: the teacher touches objects and parts of the room and children shout the name.

- Name tag: the teacher holds up pieces of equipment or apparatus and the children shout the name.

- Reverse name tag: all three of the above, except the teacher calls out the key word and a child's name and that child has to run and tag the named item or person.

- Drawing simple diagrams from the board, a book, or a handout and colouring them or labelling them or both.

- Producing an illustration for something that has been taught, if there is a bilingual speaker to explain in first language.

- Dot-to-dot: illustrations of what is being learnt, writing of their own name in its English form, tracing of current key words with illustrations to aid interpretation.

- Tracing of writing of their own name in its English form, the alphabet, numbers from one to where they have reached, days of the week, months of the year, current key words, and so forth.

- Colouring their own name card, front and back.

- Watching a video clip that supports the learning.

- Standing and stretching, arm, hand, and leg exercises.

- Marching while chanting: the alphabet, numbers to X, class names in order of seating or in alphabet order, days of the week repeated, months of the year repeated, etc.

Early Teaching Approaches

The teacher's priority in the early weeks of a new school or the first weeks of schooling for new pupils must be to embed the routines, the information, and the key words and knowledge needed for all pupils to be safe, to feel safe, and to progress with confidence as their English grows and develops. Thus, these words should be taught over and over in as many lessons and situations as the teacher can think of.

1. Key words are the simplest form of noun or verb that can be identified for effective learning.

2. If there is a word in first language that is similar in meaning, it should be used in parallel.

3. Key words do not change until pupils are confident in their knowledge of the original word and its meaning.

4. Key words are in constant use throughout initial learning and are regularly referred back to in future learning.

5. Key words that have been identified as being essential for all classes within a year group or phase should be identified on curriculum planning, but teachers should be aware that they will be generating more key words as teaching progresses.

6. For the first weeks with a new class, keep the number of key words targeted to a manageable number and keep the teaching around them simple and clear with translation whenever possible.

7. Key words are not for spelling tests, however the scribing of key words on labels and diagrams is an important part of the embedding process. When independent correct spelling does become a priority, the five 'S' system for spelling *(see Chapter 5 - The 5 'S' System for Spelling)* is highly effective for complex words for bilingual (and all) learners.

When teaching key words and other vital, early information do remember that constant repetition is the solution, but this should be executed in as many varied, interesting, and fun ways as possible.

> Trace it, dot-to-dot it, colour it, draw with a fingertip on a tactile surface and – above all – make it physical: say it, sing it, chant it, march it, dance it, stomp it, sway it, swing it, shout it, jump it.

Do anything you can think of with it!

> And above all, make the days as relaxed and pleasurable as possible.

Chapter 10 – Games, Activities, and Examples

Learning to use sophisticated sentence and language structures correctly within Standard English through fun games and activities is a tried and tested system that has consistently proved popular and highly effective. The humour and pace holds attention for all children and provides a hook for remembering the learning within.

You may wish to use the five 'S' system for spelling for learning new suave words *(see Chapter 5 - The 5 'S' System for Spelling).*

Games and Activities

Be a Suave Speaker

Oral

- Given a simple sentence in Standard English, children *suave it up* orally. They may discuss their ideas in twos or threes first.
- Given a simple sentence in dialect or local speak, children convert to Standard English and *suave it up* orally.
- Children may write between one and three sentences about current learning in any subject, convert to suave speak, and read to the class in suave speak voice. They may discuss their ideas in twos or threes first.
- Children may give a short speech in suave speak about what was learned in the lesson.
- Children may give a short speech about what they now know about X (e.g. polar bears).
- Children may give a short speech about their favourite thing, in suave speak.

Be a Suave Writer

Oral, whiteboards or paper

- Given a simple sentence in Standard English, children *suave it up* in writing and then share. They may discuss their ideas in twos or threes first.
- Given a simple sentence in dialect or local speak, children convert to Standard English and *suave it up* in writing, and then share. They may discuss their ideas first.
- Children may complete activities as in the first two bullets, but with a short paragraph of three or more sentences.

- Children may write between one and three sentences about current learning in any subject and convert to suave speak. Exchange with a friend – support each other to *suave it up* if needed. They may then read the friend's writing to the class in their suave speak voice.
- Children may *suave up*:
  - the last piece of writing they did.
  - the first paragraph of the last piece of writing they did.
  - the last paragraph of the last piece of writing they did.
  - the opening paragraph for the next piece of writing they are going to do, etc.

Big It Up Suave Speak

Oral

Children make up an exaggerated or untrue piece of news and report it in suave speak.

E.g. *'The Queen dropped into my abode for a tasty cup of tea and the use of my toilet facilities.'; 'Justin Bieber paid me the honour of a brief visit last night and invited me to appear at the annual award ceremony as a special guest.'; 'On Saturday, I was delighted to be invited to take part in the trials for the Olympics, and I am thrilled to say my performance was superb and I was awarded first place.'*

Bud's Work

Oral, whiteboard

'Bud' is an imaginary member of the class. He often makes the same mistakes in his work that real children in the class are making. Thus, their self-esteem is protected as they learn through helping Bud to get his work right by sharing suggestions. He also makes mistakes in answering questions in oral sessions and the teacher tells the class what he said. They suggest what he should have said.

- Teacher puts up Bud's work with no punctuation; in pairs or individually punctuate it.
- Teacher asks children: *'Can you create an opportunity for…?'* (Name suave punctuation to be inserted into the piece.)
- Teacher puts up Bud's work written at a simple standard; children work in pairs or individually to *suave it up*.
- Teacher puts up Bud's work with grammar errors; children work in pairs or individually to correct.
- Teacher puts up Bud's work written in dialect or in local speak; children work individually or in pairs to convert to Standard English.
- Teacher puts up Bud's work with spelling errors; children identify the errors and correct them.
- Teacher puts up a wonderful piece of writing by Bud (or another class member) and asks children to shout out the suave features line by line, or to underline them.

Call My Bluff

Oral, whiteboard

- Teacher gives a recently met suave word and three possible meanings. Children guess the correct meaning.

E.g. gibberish:

- My favourite food is fried gibberish with chips.
- I stop listening when it is all gibberish.
- The little lambs love to gibberish in the field.

- Teacher uses the class's new suave words and three meanings for each. Which example is correct?
E.g. despise:

  - To hate something or someone.
  - To make smaller.
  - To stop spying on someone.

- Teacher gives an unpunctuated sentence and three punctuation options. Which is correct?
E.g. Go away shouted the man and don't come back

  - "Go away"! shouted the man. "and dont' come back".
  - "Go away!" shouted the man, "and don't come back."
  - "Go away!" shouted the man. "and don't come back"!

- Teacher gives a sentence with a grammar error and three possible correct forms. Which is correct?
E.g. Them were my bestest shoes.

  - Those was my best shoes.
  - Them was my best shoes.
  - Those were my best shoes.

Change the Opener Game

Oral, whiteboard

- Teacher puts a simple sentence on the whiteboard.
- Children shout different sentence openers that would work with it, or

- Teacher asks specific children for a new opener, or
- Teacher goes round the room in seating order to ask for a new opener.
- E.g. We are painting:
Now, we are painting; Tomorrow, we are painting; After lunch, we are painting; Next, we are painting; Later, we are painting; Next week, we are painting; Before science, we are painting; As well as drawing, we are painting; Instead of drawing, we are painting; etc.

Describe, Describe, Describe

Oral

- Seated in a circle on the floor or on chairs.
- Teacher sets the scene e.g. *'You are in a wood; on the beach; at a party, etc.'*
- Children discuss and the teacher says *'Describe, describe, describe.'*
- Children talk, plan, feed back to the class.
- Teacher chooses one and goes round the circle. Each child adds a describing word or short phrase.

Describe Me

Oral

- Given a picture of something beautiful, weird, or scary, children describe it vividly in two or three sentences using suave features. They may discuss their ideas in twos or threes first.

- Children share their ideas with the class.
- Class work together to *suave it up*, if appropriate.
- In pairs, one partner wears a headband with a picture or named animal stuck on the front; the other partner describes what is on the card and the first partner has to guess what it is.

The Dictionary / Thesaurus Game

Oral, dictionaries or thesauruses

- Children race to find a word given orally by the teacher, in either dictionaries or thesauruses – as instructed. They shoot their hands up when finished in an effort to be first.
- The winning child gives the page number and reads out the word and definition or synonyms.
- Class locate the word and read it out.
- If a new or nearly new word, children use the five 'S' system for spelling *(see Chapter 5 - The 5 'S' System for Spelling)*.
- The class play *make me up* simple sentences to use the word e.g.
    - distraught.
    - perplexed.
    - transfixed.
    - The suave word that means (give definition).
    - A synonym for the word.
    - An antonym for the word.
- The session ends by children making up a sentence about something they are learning about, using the new word they liked best.

Fastest Finger First

Oral, paragraph on table

Fastest to point to:
- A suave opener.
- A suave verb.
- A double dash parenthesis.
- An example of a simile, etc.

Fastest Shout First

Oral

Usually in response to the teacher. E.g.
- Making deliberate mistakes when using a code of speech.
- Using a new suave word in context.
- Spotting mistakes in writing.
- Guessing the meaning of something.

Make Me Up

Oral, whiteboard

Maintain a brisk pace with humour when appropriate. Children work in twos or threes to make up sentences that include the given suave word or feature.
- *Make me up* a sentence with a given suave word (extension could be to turn the whole sentence into suave speak).
- *Make me up* a rhetorical question to follow this sentence.
- *Make me up* a suave character description of X (in response to a story stimulus or learning in history).
- *Make me up* a suave location description of X (in response to a story stimulus or learning in geography).

- *Make me up* an extended sentence using a suave connective.
- *Make me up* a sentence with direct speech.
- *Make me up* a sentence with dialect.
- *Make me up* a sentence with parenthesis.
- *Make me up* a sentence with a given suave sentence opener.
- *Make me up* a sentence with any suave sentence opener.
- *Make me up* a sentence with a literary feature e.g. simile, metaphor, etc.

A suave sentence has any two of the five suave sentence features: suave word, suave sentence opener, suave connective, suave punctuation, and literary features.

This game is also ideal for all the 'waiting times' between lessons and during breaks. When the class have finished tidying their tables before a change of lesson venue (e.g. for PE), a break, lunchtime, or at the end of the day there are often a few minutes spare and in many classrooms this is often not enough time to be utilised productively. The children could have some pleasure and accomplishment by playing an extra game such as *make me up*.

Match the Meaning

Oral, whiteboards or paper

Given a short list of suave words and the correct list of definitions in random order, children sort the two lists so that the correct definition is either beside or joined by a line to the correct suave word.

E.g.

despise	glamorous and well dressed
irate	carry on with
elegant	dislike very much
resume	extremely angry

Pictures of the Week

Oral, pictures, writing materials

- Teacher collects pictures of interesting or unusual events, ideas, characters, etc. Pobble 365 is an excellent resource for this.
- In twos or threes, children discuss responses. What might this be? What might be happening? Why might this be like this? etc.
- Children make up suave sentences to describe content.
- Children write a paragraph creatively, using the pictures as a stimulus.
- Teacher displays the pictures as prompts and for future use.

Pobble 365 was created to make it easy for busy teachers to get their pupils engaged and excited about writing. What started in a single classroom is now used by teachers from 160 countries and inspires over a million children to write each month! It was also named in Waitroses's 6 websites to keep children happy! You can find it on Pobble.com

Scrambled Suave Words

Oral, whiteboards

- Teacher puts up between three and six recently introduced suave words in scrambled form.

- Children work in pairs or individually to unscramble; teacher gives clues if needed.
- Class use the five 'S' system for spelling with unscrambled words if needed.
- E.g. massetticy – systematic; uvase – suave.
- The class need to know the suave word well and have been using it for a while.

Snap Games

Oral, cards or lists

- May be played with playing cards, on the computer, or with matching lists (one scrambled).
- Schools may make matching packs of assorted suave words. 10 cards for young children and between 20 and 30 for older children to play snap.
- Teacher shuffles the matching packs into one larger pack.
- Teacher places the large pack face down on the table top.
- Children turn the cards one by one.
- Children race to shout 'snap' when two matching cards are turned in sequence.
- The group think of as many words that mean the same or similar to the matched cards as they can.
- Children use the matched words in sentences (play *make me up*).
- Children use the five 'S' system for spelling if necessary.
- Children put the matched pair of cards to one side.
- Children shuffle the remaining cards and play again.
- Can be used with various types of words e.g. sight words, synonyms, antonyms, suave words, etc.

Spot the Difference

Oral, whiteboard

Two sections of text or paragraphs on the same subject with:
- one written in suave speak and one in plain Standard English, or
- one written in Standard English and one in phonetic local speak (words distorted by the local accent should be spelt phonetically e.g. 'et' for 'ate'), or
- one written in Standard English and one in phonetic dialect e.g. *'Us wos gobbin' us snack darn.'*

Children work in two or threes to do any one or more of the following activities:
- Compare the two pieces of text.
- Identify any differences in grammar, wording, structure, or punctuation.
- Identify any differences in meaning due to word changes between the two pieces.
- Pick out words to explore meanings.
- Use the five 'S' system for spelling to learn one or two suave words from the writing.
- Play *make me up* with the suave word/s learnt or with other interesting words in the pieces.
- Count how many different sorts of punctuation have been used in each piece.
- Identify whether there is anywhere where an exclamation mark could have been used (or ellipsis, or a dash).
- Discuss how children could create a rhetorical question in the middle or at the end of the paragraph to demonstrate a question mark (teach the term rhetorical question: a question which does not require an answer and is a literary feature).

- Identify which features make the second text more sophisticated than the first.
- Children say which they like best and why.

Spot the Small Words

Oral, whiteboards or paper

- Teacher puts up a longer word, it may be suave or it may not.
- Children see how many true words of three letters or more they can make by using letters from the word.
- Children may work in twos or threes, at the teacher's discretion.
- Letters may only be used as many times as they occur in the word.
- E.g. systematic: set, sat, sit, same, stem, scam, say, sty, mat, met, mist, mitt, may, mate, messy, time, team, test, taste, etc.
- E.g. geography: gag, gap, hag, hog, hop, her, hear, gear, hope, gape, page, year, yore, yap, peg, pog, page, etc.
- This can be played with suave words that are still being embedded.

Suave Sentences

Oral, whiteboard

- Suave sentences have any two or more of the five suave features (suave words, suave sentence openers, suave connectives, suave punctuation, and literary features).
- Children play in twos or threes.
- Children play *make me up* when given two different suave features to make up sentences that have both in.

Openers	Words/punctuation
anxiously	fraught
fortunately	aggressive
believing	()
dashing	obstruction
during	...
contrary to	robust

E.g. The fraught boy watched anxiously for his father. Fortunately, the postman escaped from the aggressive dog unharmed.

- The teacher might give the subject (from across the curriculum) that the suave sentence has to be about.
- Children play *suave it up*. Give simple sentences about learning across the curriculum and children suave them up in pairs by inserting suave features.

Suave It Up

Oral, whiteboard, whiteboards or paper

- Teacher puts one or more simple sentences on the whiteboard, read in twos. Class read together.
- In twos or threes, children discuss how the 'voice' of the sentence could be made more sophisticated by inserting suave features. Younger children will be prompted by the teacher e.g. *'Can you find another word for 'said'?'; 'Can you put a describing word* (an adverb) *in front of ran?'*
- In twos or threes, children write, or agree orally, a more sophisticated sentence.
- Children either record on small whiteboards or paper and share, or put their hands up and share, the teacher records on the whiteboard.
- All read and discuss the suggestions. Children say whether they can be improved?

Children improve simple sentences by doing one or more of the following (instructed by teacher):

- *Suave up* the verb.
- *Suave up* the adjective.
- *Suave up* the adverb.
- *Suave up* the noun by using an adjective with it.
- *Suave up* the verb by using an adverb with it.
- *Suave up* the punctuation by creating opportunity for an exclamation mark.
- *Suave up* the punctuation by creating a rhetorical question at the end.
- *Suave up* the punctuation by creating parenthesis.
- *Suave up* the sentence with a suave sentence opener.
- *Suave up* the sentence by using a suave word within it.
- *Suave up* the sentence by building one of the literary features into it. (The teacher may choose to just name one feature e.g. metaphor, or two alternatives, or give the class free choice).

Suave It Up with the Long and the Short of It

Oral, whiteboards

This game is particularly important for children aged 8 to 12.

The long and the short of it is a game to teach and embed the practice of introducing contrast at strategic points in a piece of writing by deliberately using extremely short and snappy sentences, either in succession or directly after a complex sentence.

When children understand the concept of *suave it up*, it is important to explain that not all sentences should be *suaved up*, that too many suave features can be as bad as none, and that, equally, too many suave sentences can be as bad as none. Point out that a short, simple sentence can be an excellent contrast to a complex one.

Put one or two suave sentences on the board. Discuss them and make up a snappy contrast together. This now becomes a regular game, with children given a suave sentence and asked to discuss and agree a snappy long and short of it.

- Teacher puts a complex sentence on the whiteboard.
- In twos or threes, children make up a snappy short sentence to follow it.
- Teacher puts a short, snappy sentence on the whiteboard.
- In twos or threes, children make up a complex sentence with suave features to precede it.
- When ready, children may be given between three and six examples to complete. E.g.
  - *'Desperately, I clung to the overhanging bough of the willow tree as the raging foam dragged me down. The bough broke! I hurtled...'*
  - *'Roaring and spluttering, the huge beast launched itself at the petrified gang of soldiers. They fled! We leapt at the creature...'*
  - *'Wondrous patterns formed on the velvet lawn as the burning sun burst through the dense canopy of leaves. I gazed in awe. Never had I seen...'*

Suave Slogans

Oral, IT and paper

- Class discuss what a slogan is, look at examples online and in magazines, advertisements, etc.
- The teacher or the children download GIFs, emojis, cartoons, and similar with characters doing different activities or with different facial expressions.
- Children play games and have fun making up slogans and captions for different examples that include a suave word.
- Children make up alliterative slogans e.g. Fiery Fred the Fireman.
- Children make up onomatopoeic slogans e.g. Clickety Click the Cricket.
- Children make up simile slogans e.g. As Swift as a Sprint.
- Each pupil researches and downloads a chosen cartoon or emoji (or actually designs their own in art) and creates three different captions, each with a suave word.
- The class display their ideas and read each other's.

Suave Subjects

Oral, IT and paper

- The teacher chooses geographical features e.g. a capital city or city of culture in a country that has been studied or is about to be studied, a country, ocean, sea, continent, the lines of latitude. They do all work in geography time, or
- The teacher chooses historical locations e.g. Rome, Egypt, The Amazon Rainforest, Dunkirk, The Caribbean, The Soldier's Leap, St Paul's Cathedral, Australia, etc. Do all work in history time.
- Children undertake own research and draft a report for an encyclopaedia.
- Children work in twos to *suave up* both their pieces of writing.
- Children produce a drawing or map on new paper.
- Children copy their finished piece in best handwriting below or around the illustration or map.

Suave Super Heroes

Oral, IT and paper

- Each child chooses one famous person from each of two or three areas of the curriculum e.g. an explorer, a scientist, an inventor, an artist, an athlete, a sportsman, a leader from the past, a hero from the past, a writer, a poet, etc.
- Children use speech bubbles to create a snappy exchange of words and statements between the two or three. Include at least one suave word or suave feature in each. E.g. Dr Livingstone or Henry the Eighth; Thomas Edison or Florence Nightingale.

  For example:
  Lewis Howard Latimer: *Mr Edison, I have a long and fearsome journey to go on.*
  Edison: *Worry not Sir, I shall surely be your guiding light.*
  Lewis Howard Latimer: *Nay, Mr Edison, your light would have guided no-one without my own invention of the filament!*

- Research appearances and produce an illustration of the pair with cartoon-type speech bubbles (which might be light bulb shaped as a touch of humour) either through art or technology.

- Children make up alliterative or simile or onomatopoeic slogans or captions for them.

Suave Word Search

Paper, IT or whiteboards

Teachers make up word searches on paper or digitally, with all suave words the class are currently working on as the hidden words.

- Children work alone or in pairs to find and mark each suave word as they find it.
- Children write the meanings into the empty line left after each word in the list of words to find.
- Children play *make me up* using the suave words.

Suave Word of the Week

Homework books or similar

- Teachers develop a programme of powerful words to be given to the class, one at a time, or use the word of the week resource from our website. For examples, *see page 123.*
- The class use the five 'S' spelling system to learn the word.
- Class use the words in games and activities.
- Teacher displays new words and use constantly across the curriculum.

Synonym Saviours

Oral, whiteboard, whiteboards or paper

Teacher puts a short piece on the whiteboard or on paper, with one word used repeatedly. E.g. *'The sun shone on the hot beach. The children were so hot they wanted to go in the sea to avoid the hot sun. "We are hot, Mummy," said the children. "Please take us into the sea to get off the hot beach."'*

- Read aloud together.
- Children spot the repeated word.
- Children work in twos or threes to make a list of as many synonyms for that word as they can.
- When they run out of ideas, they could use a thesaurus if able, to find some more or whole class share and collect more ideas.
- Children work in twos or threes to change as many instances of the repeated word as they are able into new words.
- Children read their piece through to check it.
- Children should be prepared to read it to another group or the class.
- E.g. *'The sun shone on the burning beach. The children were so hot they wanted to go in the sea to avoid the heat of the day. "We are baking, Mummy," said the children. "Please take us into the sea to get off this scorching beach."'*

Which Word Works?

Oral, whiteboard

- The teacher puts some sentences with a space for an adjective, adverb, verb, or connective, on the whiteboard.
- The teacher gives examples of known suave words circling, zooming in or out, or just listed.
- In twos or threes, children work out which words would fit in which sentences so that each word is used only once and all sentences make sense.
- All share ideas and discuss meanings.
- Older children should be told that one word may be an unknown, so leave that until last. Which sentence must it go in when all the others are complete?
- In twos or threes, children now guess the meaning of the unknown word from the context.
- If time, children play *fastest finger first* to find the meaning in the dictionary, if not the teacher confirms the meaning.
- Teacher scribes the word large by itself and leads the class in its use of the five 'S' system for spelling.
- The whole class play *make me up* sentences on different issues to do with current learning that include the new word. If insufficient time for this in this session, play in different subjects as they occur on the timetable throughout the week.

Word Shout

Oral, whiteboard

- Must be played at speed. Teacher shows a simple noun, verb, or adjective and then calls names round the class in seating or alphabet order. Children should respond with either synonyms, antonyms, or alliteration, depending on which has been asked for.
- The named child shouts an answer before teacher has counted to five out loud.
- If the named child does not succeed, another name is called.
- If the second child doesn't succeed, the teacher asks if anyone has one.
- The last child to name an appropriate word scores a point.
- Teacher shows a list of all the appropriate words they have found. Children read all.
- The class play *make me up* with any words totally new to all.
- Teacher shows the next word and restarts the names where the last game ended.

Exemplar Introductory Activities for Talk:Write Sessions

The following provides two different activities suitable for introducing code switching in Talk:Write for children in each of three age groups. Children should have already experienced the discussion activities described for introducing the five codes of speech, *(see Chapter 3 – The 5 Codes of Speech)*.

Consider performing several of these types of activities in assemblies or at parents' evenings and explaining what they demonstrate.

Age 4 to 7

This may also make a good introductory activity for older children.

Spend 10 to 15 minutes a day for three to five days.

Example 1

1. As a class, read and recite the nursery rhyme *Little Miss Muffet*.
2. Discuss which of the two characters (Miss Muffet and the spider) might speak in suave speak and which in local speak.
3. Work in twos. Have fun playing with suave versions of what Miss Muffet might say to the spider and what the spider might reply in local speak. Teacher circulates and picks one or two examples for performance.

4. Choose a popular one and work together as a class to improve both Miss Muffet's speeches and the spider's speeches. Record on the whiteboard.
5. Children practise in pairs. They may change speeches as they wish.
6. Public performances for fun to the class, year, or school.

Miss Muffet: (sitting on tuffet with a bowl of curds and whey) *Well, good afternoon, Mr Spider. How perfectly delightful to see you here today.*

Mr Spider: (ambling sideways on all fours towards the tuffet) *Aye up, Miss M. Cool ter si thee too. Ah reckon ah'll jus' climb up beside thee and share thar snap.*

Miss Muffet: (snatching bowl up high and recoiling in dismay) *Oh NO, Mr Spider! Young ladies of charm do not mix with spiders like you. How absolutely frightful! Go away – pray go away!* (Flaps her hand at him.)

Mr Spider: (climbing up on the tuffet and seizing the bowl, burying his head in it) *Mmm... this is yummy, Miss M. Ah wus jus' ready fer a snack!*

Miss Muffet: (holding hands up in horror) *Oh how completely ghastly! A spider in my curds and whey! I shall hasten home to report all to Mama immediately!* (Runs away)

Mr Spider: (looks up with a grin and wipes one arm across mouth) *Bah gum – sure is great fun bein' a spider and yer gets loads ter eat!*

Example 2

1. Bianca and Bella are arguing. Can you spot which one is using local speak and which one is speaking in suave speak?
2. What are they arguing about?
3. Can you change the two characters over so that they continue their conversation using the opposite form of talk?
4. Can you role play the two girls having a squabble about how they talk, with one using local speak and the other using suave speak.

Bianca: *I's tired of yer bossin' us abaht, Bella. Leave us alone why don't yer?*

Bella: *I am not bossing you, Bianca. I am trying to help Mummy. She wants you to behave nicely.*

Bianca: *Yer not me mam, Bella, so leave us alone...*

Bella: *Good manners are important to Mummy, Bianca, and she wants you to speak correctly – as I do.*

Bianca: *Yer just a creep, Bella. When us is playin' art yer talks just like't rest o' us.*

Bella: *And that, my dear sister, is just the point. We need to be able to change the way we speak to match the situation we are in.*

Age 6 to 10

Spend four to five short sessions (10 to 15 minutes long) throughout the week on oral Talk:Write.

Example 1

1. Teach the differences between suave speak and local speak as for the examples for children aged four to seven.
2. Practise short quotations and phrases.
3. Find pictures that will interest or engage.
4. In *Bonkers Boris Meets the Mayor*, Boris is talking with the mayor. Who do you think will be talking in suave speak and who will be talking in local speak?
5. Working in pairs, make up a short dialogue using the two kinds of talk. Rehearse and perform.

Mayor: *Aye up lad, 'oo're you?*

Boris: *My name is Boris, Sir Mayor.*

Mayor: *Nay lad, jus' call me Mr Mayor, or jus' Ned...*

Boris: *Thank you Sir, Mr Ned.*

Mayor: *An' what canst ah do fer thee, lad?*

Boris: *Well, if you please Sir Mr Ned, I wish to be famous when I reach adulthood. Might it be possible for such an important gentleman as yourself to give me some small hints on how that might come about?*

Mayor: *Nay, lad, thar jus' lives thee life ter't best yer can an' if yer do... mebbe folks'll notice thee.*

**Bonkers Boris Meets the Mayor
(Ros Wilson, 2020)**

Example 2

1. Can you change the two characters over so that they continue their conversation using the opposite form of talk?
2. Can you role play the two characters having a squabble about how they

talk, with one using local speak and the other using suave speak?

Miss Prim: *Good afternoon, Sir, how charming to meet you during this somewhat stormy sunset!*

Mr Moo: *Aye up, lass, 'ow are thee?*

Miss Prim: *Perfectly wonderful, Mr Moo, thank you. And how might you be?*

Mr Moo: *Ahm reet grand thanks. Now shift theesen so ah canst gerra bit o' grazin' done.*

Miss Prim: *My dear friend, you really do need to practise talking correctly. A handsome beast of your size should have the most impressive speech.*

Mr Moo: *Ah talks as I wants, lass – and don't thee forget it. Now shift yersen.*

Miss Prim: *I shall, and I won't be pausing to chat with you again. So rude!*

Age 8 to 12

Address one text sample per session across four sessions in the first week (four different texts) or two in the first week and two in the second week, with code switching practice in between. Excerpts from stories the class have enjoyed are good for this, if they provide sections of dialogue that may be used. Alternatively, the children could make up dialogues between two of the most interesting characters, writing one in local speak and one in Standard English. They could then exchange characters in their readings in role.

Example 1

1. Name the two giraffes e.g. 'Mother G' and 'Baby G' or ask students to name them something else.
2. Ask students to discuss what sort of conversation they might have as they enjoy their day.
3. Ask students to make up a model conversation to use to entertain younger children, with one giraffe speaking suave speak and one speaking local speak.

Mother G: *Now my dear child, there's an aeroplane – it is something you would really do rather better to stay away from.*

Baby G: *Blimey, Mum, thassa big un!*

Mother G: *Now, I have asked you not to speak like that, darling. It is perfectly acceptable when you are playing with friends but not when you are with your father and myself. How should you have phrased that?*

Baby G: (Looks at her puzzled) *Erm… cor blimey, Mummy, thassa a big un!*

Mother G: *Sweetheart, we just do not ever say 'blimey' or 'cor blimey'. What does one iterate when one is surprised?*

Baby G: *Erm… crikey?*

Mother G: *Oh, I do despair… one might usually say 'gosh' or 'golly'. Please remember that.*

Baby G: *Gosh yes, I will. Golly blimey, Mummy, thassa a big un. Is it a bee or a wasp or a mosquito? Yer look like yer's gunna ge'r'it!*

Mother G: *No, my baby, it is not. That is a machine built by humans to move people around the world. It is called an aeroplane and it can travel very quickly.*

Baby G: *Eeeh, mah giddy ant! Who'd o' thort it?*

Example 2

1. Meet sister and brother, Daisy-Mae and Junior. Your job is to make up a conversation between the two children with one speaking in suave speak and one in local speak. This must be used in a lesson to be taught to five to six-year-olds to explain the differences in the two types of speech.
2. Can you change the two characters over so that they continue their conversation using the opposite form of talk?

3. Can you role play the two children having a squabble about how they talk, with one using local speak and the other using suave speak?

Junior: *Aye up, Daisy-Mae, can ah ave sum o' thee pocket money ter get sum sweets?*

Daisy-Mae: *Well hello, Junior, how lovely to see you here. Actually, I am just popping to the store to buy a few necessities.*

Junior: *Well gee us sum cash fust eh?*

Daisy-Mae: *How frightfully you do speak, but I suppose I could give you ten pence to spend as you wish.*

Junior: *TEN PENCE? That won't buy owt thah knows, ah needs 't'least a pound.*

Daisy-Mae: *Well I am most terribly sorry, Junior, but I need my small allowance to purchase my necessities. You will have to ask Mother to give you your own allowance if you want more.*

Junior: *Thar's a reet mean 'un, Daisy-Mae. Ah'll not be sharin' me stash o' sweets wit' thee thar knows...*

Exemplar Texts in the Range of Codes of Speech

Use for translation, comparison, modelling, and analysis.

Example 1: My Pet

Standard English

I have a small dog called Ruff. He is a mixed-breed with fluffy, brown hair. Ruff is often naughty. He steals slippers and bits of clothing. He often chews these up or runs away and hides them.

Local Speak

I 'av' a small dog. 'Is name's Ruff an' 'e is a mix wi' fluffy, brown 'air. Our Ruff's norty an' 'e steals slippers an' stuff. 'E chews 'em up or 'ides them in't garden.

Dialect

Sithee – us 'as a 'ickle dog. 'Ees Ruff an' 'ees mixt wit' brown locks. Us Ruff's fair wick an' 'e nicks us stuff.

Suave Speak

Our family pet is named Ruff. He is an adorable little cross-breed with shaggy, brown fur and huge amber eyes. Mischief is his middle name and he frequently steals our personal possessions and destroys them or spirits them away to who knows where!

Example 2: My Hobby

Standard English

My hobby is running. I go for runs with my friends and with my father. We run round the park or along the lane by the railway. I like running because it makes me fit.

Local Speak

Me 'obby's runnin'. I go fer runs wit' me friends an' me dad. We run round't park or dahn't lane by't railway. It meks me fit.

Dialect

Us 'obby's runnin'. Us goes wit' me mates an me da'. Us goes rown't park an' dahn't snicket by't train track thar knows.

Suave Speak

I have many hobbies, but my preferred pastime is probably running. My friends, my father, and I frequently run round the local park or along the leafy lane beside the rail track. Running relaxes me and also makes me fit, it is a wonderful hobby.

Example 3: My Favourite Food

Standard English

My favourite food is a cheeseburger. If mum gives me a choice, I like to go to the burger bar and have a cheeseburger with chips and a milkshake. I eat them really quickly because they are delicious.

Local Speak

Me best food's a cheese burger. I luvs it when mum teks me ter 't'burger bar. I 'av' a burger an' chips an' I fair wolf 'em down 'cos they're smashin'.

Dialect

Ay'oop. Me bessie nosh is't burger 'n' fries when't mam teks us ter't burger bar. Them's lush an' ah scoffs 'em dahn.

Suave Speak

Normally, I choose to eat healthily, enjoying salads and pasta, however I do have a secret weakness and that is a cheeseburger. The ultimate burger for me is made by my parents when they light the barbecue. I like the thick meat patties my mother makes, smothered in cheese with lettuce and tomato slices. Juices dribble down my chin as I devour this secret sin.

Examples of a Talk:Write Week

The following are examples. The day, time, and games used might be different. There are a range of games provided earlier in this chapter. One of the five weekly sessions is for refreshing and planning immediately before the suave writing session.

For a reminder of how to timetable the weekly sessions, *(see Chapter 2 - Launching Talk:Write).*

Age 4 to 7

Session 1

Monday: After playtime for 10 minutes

- **Make Me Up:** Teacher says, *'Make me up a sentence about what you did on Saturday morning, opening with the words "On Saturday morning," It may not be true.'* For example, you might say: *'On Saturday morning, the Queen popped in for a cup of tea.'*
- **Share:** Round your group or table.
- **Share:** An interesting sentence you heard from a friend on your table with the whole class.
- **Teacher Q and A:** How many of you used an adjective or adverb (describing word for young children) in your sentence? Not applicable for four to five-year-olds.
- **Suave It Up:** Teacher says, *'Improve your sentence by inserting a suave feature (suave word, suave opener, or suave punctuation) and re-share. Suggest and discuss ideas with friends. Share finished sentences.'* Teacher selects one of the suave words heard or suggests a

new one, explains it, and the children try it in sentences.

- **5 'S' System for Spelling:** Focus on one suave word that caught attention, or the teacher gives a new example relevant to one of the children's contributions. Discuss the meaning. Use the five 'S' system for spelling to embed it *(see Chapter 5 - The 5 'S' System for Spelling).*
- **Make Me Up:** Play using the new word.

Session 2

Tuesday: After lunch for 10 to 15 minutes

- **Spot the Difference:** Two or three sentences on the whiteboard or flipchart. As a class, led by the teacher, discuss how they are the same and how they are different.

'The little girl ran through the wood. She was frightened. She thought there was a bear.'

'Quickly, the frightened little girl fled through the gloomy wood. She really believed there might be a big, scary bear in there.'

Pick out the suave features. Do the children understand why they are called suave?

- Suave sentence opener and adverb for description of how the girl moved – 'Quickly'.
- Suave verb – 'fled'.
- Suave adjective – 'gloomy'.
- Suave adverb – 'really', etc.
- Teacher focuses on 'big, scary bear'. What is suave about this? Two adjectives in a list and use of a comma.

- **As a class:** How many synonyms can we find for 'big'? Teacher records on the whiteboard. E.g. massive, huge, enormous, gigantic, large. If not suggested, teacher suggests a new one e.g. colossal or immense and adds to the list. Children choose the suave word they like best and exchange it for 'big' in the sentence.
- **Make Me Up:** Children make up their own sentences (may be in twos or threes) about something scary in the wood, using the new word for 'big' that they like the best.
- **Teacher Q and A:** Did any new sentence have a suave opener? Did anyone use the word 'fled'? Did anyone use any other suave words they are pleased with?

Session 3

Wednesday: For 15 minutes after registration or before assembly or in a geography lesson

- **Suave It Up:** The teacher asks, *'Can you and a friend make the following much more interesting by adding suave features?'* e.g. a suave sentence opener, an adjective, and ? or ! for six plus. The following might be given to either age group:

'We are learning about polar bears in geography. They live inside the Arctic Circle and they eat meat. Polar bears are big.'

Children aged five plus may suggest inserting 'amazing' before polar bears; they may remember one of their synonyms for 'big' from the previous session. The teacher might re-show the list of synonyms they made. In twos or threes, *suave up* the sentence.

'In geography, we are learning about amazing polar bears. These huge animals live inside the Arctic Circle and they are meat eaters.'

- **Codes of Speech:** The teacher scribes a sentence in local speak on the board and asks the children to read it aloud together twice. Then children work in twos or threes to change it to Standard English.

'Nowt much live in't Arctic Cercle 'cept 't' polar bear but seals an reindeer does.'

Children make oral suggestions to change the sentence into Standard English and the teacher records the new sentence on the whiteboard.

'Not many animals live in the Arctic Circle besides the polar bear, but seals and reindeer are two that do.'

- **Suave It Up:** Teacher asks children to make suggestions for how the sentence could be *suaved up*. Teacher scribes on whiteboard when all are agreed. Everyone reads both sentences, one after the other.

'Very few animals live inside the Arctic Circle besides the colossal polar bear, however seals and reindeer are two that do.'

Friday: For 10 minutes before morning playtime

- **Spot the Suave Words:** Short paragraph with new suave words that are going to be useful in ongoing cross-curricular theme on air pollution.

  'When smoke or fumes go into the air they make it dirty. This is called air pollution. Air pollution can harm some plants and animals.'

- **Call My Bluff:** From discussions about the text above, which do you think is the correct definition for its use in this writing? E.g.

- fumes:
  - bits of dirt.
  - dangerous gases.
  - angry.

- pollution:
  - the people who live in a country.
  - a type of truck.
  - stuff that makes something poisonous or harmful.

- harm:
  - part of the body.
  - hurt something.
  - a field.

- **Make Me Up:** Choose one of the three below to play this game.
  - A sentence about rivers with the word pollution in.
  - A sentence about plastic bags with the word pollution in.
  - A sentence about the sky with the word pollution in.

- **Spot the Small Words:** How many true words with three letters or more can the class make together from the letters in the word 'pollution'? Explain that a letter may only be used the number of times it

occurs in the word. E.g. pit, pot, put, pin, pill, plot, lip, lot, not, nut, nip, tin, ton, tip, etc.

- **Make Me Up:** A sentence about pollution that opens with 'naturally' and has 'however' in, to help to embed previous learning.

- **Codes of Speech:** The teacher puts two sentences on the whiteboard written in local speak. The class read them out loud and then work together to change them to Standard English.

  'Us car meks 't sky mucky when't smoke cums art ot back end. Us needs a new un.'

  The teacher may have to give the word 'exhaust' if no one knows it.

  'Our car pollutes the sky when fumes come out of its exhaust. We need a new one.'

  All read the first and second versions together.

- **Suave It Up:** Discuss in twos or threes where you might add two or more suave features to *suave it up*. Share as a class. The teacher makes the changes.

  'Our battered, old car pollutes the sky when fumes pour out of its exhaust. Truly, we need a new one.'

  All read the first and last versions together.

Monday: After play for 10 to 15 minutes

- **Make Me Up:** Teacher says *'Talk about something you did on Saturday morning, opening with the words "On Saturday morning," It may not be true.'* For example, you might say:

  'On Saturday morning, the Queen popped in for a cup of tea. She asked if she could use the toilet and I directed her to the bathroom. When she'd gone I found she had left her crown on the side of the bath!'

- **Circle Time:** Class seated in a circle, children share their made up 'news'. Spot the interesting sentence! Children pick out bits they particularly liked.

- **Teacher Q and A:** *'How many of you used an adjective or adverb* (describing word for young children) *in your sentence? Did anyone hear a particularly interesting adjective?'*

- **Suave It Up:** Children choose their favourite sentence from their own or a friend's 'news'. Improve the sentence by inserting a suave feature (suave word, suave opener, or suave punctuation) and re-share. Teacher selects one of the sentences heard and suggests a new suave feature, explains it, and the children try it in their sentences.

- **5 'S' System for Spelling:** Focus on one suave word that caught attention, or the teacher gives a new example relevant to one of the children's contributions. Discuss the meaning. Use the five 'S' system for spelling to embed it *(see Chapter 5 - The 5 'S' System for Spelling).*

- **Discuss:** What the class will be doing in one or two key lessons from the foundation subjects (history, geography, art, music, PE or D and T) that day.

- **Make Me Up:** Play using the new word in a sentence about the learning to come.

Tuesday: After lunch for 10 to 15 minutes

- **Spot the Difference:** Two short paragraphs on the whiteboard. In pairs, children identify and talk through how they are the same and how they are different.

  'At lunchtime, a large, brown bear came onto the school playground. At first, we were all a bit scared but then it said it just wanted to play with us. We all had a fun game of tig.'

  'During lunchtime, an enormous, chocolate coloured bear wandered into our playground. Naturally, we were all a little frightened at first, however when it told us it only wanted to play with us, we were reassured. Then, what fun we all had playing at tig!'

- **Fastest Shout First:** An 'ly' (adverbial) suave sentence opener e.g. naturally; a suave sentence opener for time e.g. during lunchtime; a suave sentence opener for sequence e.g. then; a suave connective to extend a sentence e.g. however; suave punctuation e.g. create an opportunity for a question mark (age eight plus).

  E.g. can you create an opportunity to use a rhetorical question: *'Wouldn't you be?'* after *'...we were all a little frightened at first.'*

- **Make Me Up:** Some suave sentences using two of the suave features from the paragraphs e.g. 'naturally' and 'however'.

  'Naturally, our teacher is the best in the school. However, she is not the best singer.'

Session 3

Wednesday: For 15 minutes after registration or before assembly or in a geography lesson

- **Suave It Up:** The teacher asks, *'Can you and a friend make the following much more interesting by adding suave features?'* e.g. a suave sentence opener, an adjective, and brackets (aged eight plus only for brackets, ? or ! for six plus). The following might be given to either age group:

  'We are learning about polar bears in geography. They live inside the Arctic Circle and they eat meat. Polar bears are big.'

  Children aged six plus may suggest inserting 'amazing' before polar bears; they may remember one of their synonyms for 'big' from the previous session. The teacher might re-show the list of synonyms they made.

  In twos or threes, *suave up* the sentence.

  'In geography, we are learning about incredible polar bears. These colossal animals live inside the Arctic Circle and they are meat eaters.'

- **Codes of Speech:** The teacher scribes a sentence in local speak on the board and asks the children to read it aloud together twice.

Then children work in twos or threes to change it to Standard English.

'Nowt much live in't Arctic Cercle 'cept 't' polar bear but seals an reindeers does.'

Children work in twos or threes on whiteboards to change the sentence into Standard English. All show and the teacher records an accurate version of the sentence on the whiteboard.

'Not many animals live in the Arctic Circle besides the polar bear, but seals and reindeer are two that do.'

- **Suave It Up:** Teacher asks children to work in their twos or threes to *suave up* the accurate sentence with suave features on their whiteboards. All show. The teacher scribes an accurate and enriched version on the whiteboard when all are agreed. Everyone reads both sentences, one after the other.

  'Very few animals live inside the freezing Arctic Circle, besides the colossal polar bear, however seals and reindeer are two examples that do. Which is your favourite?'

Session 4

Friday: For 10 minutes before morning playtime

- **Spot the Suave Words:** Short paragraph or complex sentence with new suave words that are going to be useful in ongoing cross-curricular theme on air pollution.

'Air pollution became a problem when the burning of coal started as a source of heat in the 13th century, but increased rapidly in the 19th century with the expansion of industrialisation.'

- **Call My Bluff:** From discussions about the text above, the teacher asks the class which they think is the correct definition for each word. Children discuss in twos or threes and then give their answers (or play *fastest shout first*).
  - source:
    - ketchup.
    - a cut in the skin.
    - the place something starts.
  - expansion:
    - to grow larger.
    - a stretch of grass.
    - a machine in a gym.
  - rapidly:
    - noisily.
    - quickly.
    - carefully.
- **Make Me Up:** Choose one of the three below to play this game.
  - A sentence about the sun with source in.
  - A sentence about rivers with the word source in.
  - A sentence about your favourite game or TV programme with the word source in.
  - The teacher asks if anyone included any suave features. Feedback.
- **Codes of Speech:** The teacher puts two sentences on the whiteboard written in local speak. The class read them out loud and then work together to change them to Standard English.

'Us car meks 't sky mucky when't smoke cums art ot back end. Us needs a new un sithee.'

The teacher may have to give the word 'exhaust' if no one knows it.

'Our car pollutes the sky when fumes come out of its exhaust. We need a new one you know.'

All read the first and second versions together.

- **Suave It Up:** Discuss in twos or threes where you might add two or more suave features to *suave it up*. Share as a class. The teacher makes the changes:

'Our battered, old vehicle pollutes the atmosphere when fumes pour out of its exhaust. Truly, we need a new one! Don't you agree?'

All read the first and last versions together.

- **Spot the Small Words:** How many true words with three letters or more can the children make from the letters in the word 'expansion', working in twos or threes. Explain that a letter may only be used the number of times it occurs in the word. Share. E.g. son, pan, pie, spin, none, pea, nose, pin, pen, snip, etc.
- **Make Me Up:** A sentence about pollution that opens with 'naturally' and has 'however' in, to help to embed previous learning.

'Naturally, everyone knows that heavy smoke from chimneys causes pollution, however many countries still have exceedingly large chimneys in use.'

Monday: After playtime for 10 to 15 minutes

- **Make Me Up:** Teacher says, *'Talk about something you did at the weekend. It may not be true.'* For example, you might say:

  'At the weekend, I was summoned to Windsor Castle to join the Royal Family for a garden party. The Queen sent her helicopter for me, and it landed on our street, right outside my house. When I arrived at the castle, there was a very large crowd and I discovered that they wanted me to perform my epic gymnastics routine. They were stunned!'

- **Circle Time:** Six children share their made up 'news' (on a weekly rota). After each shared 'news', the class:

  - Spot the interesting sentence! Children pick out a sentence they particularly liked.
  - Spot the suave word! Children identify their favourite suave word.
  - Spot the suave opener! Children identify a sentence with a suave opener.
  - Spot any other suave features. The teacher might identify what to ask for. E.g. in this example there is the opportunity for suave punctuation – the exclamation mark at the end. There is also an example of the long and the short of it, *see page 104.*

- **Teacher Q and A:** *'How many of you used a suave adjective or adverb in your own news? Did anyone use any other particularly interesting suave feature?'*

- **Suave It Up:** Teacher selects one of the sentences heard and suggests a new suave word, explains it, and the children try it in the original sentence and then in one of their own sentences.

- **5 'S' System for Spelling:** Focus on the new suave word. Discuss the meaning. Use the five 'S' system for spelling to embed it *(see Chapter 5 – The 5 'S' System for Spelling).*

- **Discuss:** What the class will be doing in one or two key lessons from the foundation subjects (history, geography, art, music, PE or D&T) that day.

- **Make Me Up:** Using the new word in a sentence about the learning to come.

Tuesday: After lunch for 10 to 15 minutes

- **Spot the Difference:** Two short paragraphs on the whiteboard. In twos or threes, children identify and talk through how they are the same and how they are different.

  'After school, a large, brown bear came into the park while we were playing football. At first, we were all a bit scared but then it said it just wanted to play with us. We all had a fun game with the bear as a goalkeeper.'

  'During the evening, an enormous, chocolate coloured bear wandered into the park and stopped to watch us playing football. Naturally, we were all a little frightened at first, however when it told us it only wanted to join in, we were reassured. Then, what fun we all had, with our huge, furry friend in goals!'

- **Fastest Shout First:** An 'ly' (adverbial) suave sentence opener e.g. naturally; a suave sentence opener for time e.g. during the evening; a suave connective to extend a sentence e.g. however; suave punctuation e.g. the exclamation mark; an example of alliteration e.g. furry friend; a suave word meaning we stopped worrying e.g. reassured.

- **Teacher Q and A:** Can you create an opportunity for a question mark? Remind the class and give an example of a rhetorical question if needed: '(wouldn't you be?)' inserted in brackets after 'frightened at first'; 'How amazing was that?' at the end.

- **Fastest Shout First:** Synonyms for 'amazing'? E.g. astonishing, astounding, surprising, etc. If no-one has suggested it, teacher offers 'incredible'. Class trial it in the sentence.

- **Make Me Up:** Suave sentences using two or more of the suave features from the paragraphs e.g. 'naturally' and 'however'. Teacher gives a subject for all e.g. 'our class'.

  'Naturally, our teacher is the best in the school – she is incredible! However, she is not the best singer!'

  Teacher asks for examples. Did anyone include a rhetorical question? Can we all add one now? E.g. *'Who is?'* at the end.

Session 3

Wednesday: For 15 minutes after registration or before assembly or in a geography lesson

- **Suave It Up:** The teacher asks, *'Can you and a friend make the following much more interesting by adding suave features? And add more information about polar bears of your own please.'* E.g. a suave sentence opener, an adjective, and brackets. The following might be given:

  'We are learning about polar bears in geography. They live inside the Arctic Circle and they eat meat. Polar bears are big.'

  In twos or threes, *suave up* the sentence.

  'In geography, we are learning about the incredible polar bear. This is the largest species of bear (and the largest land carnivore) and it lives within the Arctic Circle. Amazingly, these mighty beasts can swim continuously for several days.'

- **Codes of Speech:** The teacher scribes a sentence in local speak on the board and asks the children to read it aloud together twice. Then children work in twos or threes to change it to Standard English.

  'Nowt much live in't Arctic Cercle 'cept 't' polar bear but seals an reindeers does. Us dun't much want ter meet a polar bear cos them is reet big.'

  Children work alone or in twos or threes on whiteboards to change the sentence into Standard English. All show and the teacher records an accurate version of the sentences on the whiteboard.

  'Not many animals live in the Arctic Circle besides the polar bear, but seals and reindeer are two that do. We wouldn't much like to meet a polar bear because they are colossal.'

- **Suave It Up:** If the children did not naturally *suave up* their sentences into suave writing, the teacher asks children to work in their twos or threes to *suave* *up* the accurate sentence. The teacher scribes an accurate and enriched version on the whiteboard when all are agreed. If no-one had inserted a rhetorical question, the teacher reminds them all about how they work and asks for suggestions as to what could be asked and where it would go. The teacher adds one to the final suave version.

'Not many animals live in the Arctic Circle besides the polar bear, but seals and reindeer are two that do. We wouldn't much like to meet a polar bear because they are colossal. Would you?'

Everyone reads both sentences, the local speak and the suave writing, one after the other.

Session 4

Friday: For 10 minutes before morning playtime

- **Spot the Suave Words:** Short paragraph with new suave words that are going to be useful in ongoing cross-curricular theme on air pollution.

   'Air pollution became a problem historically with the introduction of burning coal as a source of heat in the 13th century, but increased rapidly in the 19th century with the expansion of industrialisation.'

- **Call My Bluff:** From discussions about the text above, which do you think is the correct definition?
- source:
  - ketchup.
  - a cut in the skin.
  - the place something starts.

- expansion:
  - to grow larger.
  - a stretch of grass.
  - a machine in a gym.
- rapidly:
  - noisily.
  - quickly.
  - carefully.
- industrialisation:
  - growth of factories.
  - to make clothes.
  - to work hard.
- **Make Me Up:** The teacher asks the class to choose one of the three below to play this game, inserting two or more suave features into their sentences.
  - A sentence about the sun with source in.
  - A sentence about rivers with the word source in.
  - A sentence about your favourite game or TV programme with the word source in.

- **Spot the Small Words:** How many true words with three letters or more can you make from the letters in the word 'industrialisation'? Explain that a letter may only be used the number of times it occurs in the word. E.g. din, dust, dial, sun, son, stir, list, trial, tin, ton, trod, last, etc.
- **Make Me Up:** A sentence about pollution that opens with 'naturally' and has 'however' in, to help to embed previous learning.

   'Naturally, everyone is aware that heavy smoke and fumes from industrial chimneys cause pollution, however many countries still have large chimneys in use. Isn't this appalling?'

Exemplar Homework Suave Words

The following are words that would enrich the writing of children of any age yet are within the capabilities of learning for most children aged six years and above. A wider selection of examples are available on our website.

Ideas for use:
- Look up the word in an adult dictionary or on Google.
- Look up words of similar meaning in a thesaurus or on Google.
- Use the word in three different sentences – the subject for each will be given by the teacher and when possible will relate to current learning.
- Unscramble the word into correct form when given scrambled.

1. **Abrupt / ly:** sudden and quickly, quite often when angry or surprised.
   The ending was abrupt.
2. **Giddy / Giddily:** dizzy or silly.
   I was giddy with excitement.
3. **Ecstatic:** full of joy.
   I was ecstatic when my poem was read out in assembly.
4. **Scoff / ed:** mock someone or sneer at them.
   The teacher scoffed at my drawing.
5. **Headlong:** falling headfirst or doing something without thinking about it first.
   Jonny fell headlong down the banking.
6. **Amidst:** in the middle of.
   Amidst all my new birthday clothes, I found my old jeans.
7. **Tender / ly:** be gentle with someone or something.
   The cat and I had a tender moment.

8. **Perky / perkily:** lively, saucy, or a bit cheeky.
   Her perky smile made the teacher stop being cross.
9. **Tragic / tragically:** very sad thing to happen.
   Losing my pet was tragic for me.
10. **Thrill / ed:** excite or delight.
    I was thrilled with the gift.
11. **Fogey:** a person with old-fashioned ideas.
    The old fogey told us off.
12. **Fearless / ly:** without fear.
    Fearlessly, I rushed into the classroom.

For Children Aged 8 to 12

1. **Surreptitious / ly:** sneakily and without being seen.
   He took the book surreptitiously from my bag.
2. **Appal / Appalling:** very bad or upsetting.
   His behaviour was appalling.
3. **Disastrous / ly:** terrible or very bad.
   Everything went wrong – it was disastrous!
4. **Persuade / d:** make someone want to do something.
   I was persuaded to go to the party.
5. **Deride / d:** put down or make unimportant.
   She derided that idea and used her own.
6. **Lament / ed:** Mourn for someone or be very sorry.
   I lamented over my lost pet.
7. **Ferocious / ly:** very angry or vicious.
   It attacked the dog ferociously.
8. **Glamorous / ly:** very attractive and elegant.
   The film star was very glamorous.

9. **Ascend / ing:** rising upwards.
   The smoke was ascending from the chimney.

10. **Jovial / ly:** very jolly and cheerful.
    The smiling woman greeted us jovially.

11. **Derelict:** ruined, unused for many years.
    The boy hid in the derelict shed.

12. **Vigorous / ly:** very energetically.
    She shook the rug vigorously to get rid of crumbs.

Exemplar Homework Topics

1. The best day of your life...
2. The worst day of your life...
3. The most famous person you have met...
4. Someone you would really like to meet...
5. Your favourite television programmes / stars...
6. What you would do if you won a million pounds...
7. What change would you most like to make in this school / this locality / this city / this country...
8. The best holiday you ever had...
9. The best day out you ever had...
10. A place you would really like to go...
11. A job you would really like to have...
12. The best neighbour you ever had...
13. Your best friend...
14. Your best ever present...
15. Your favourite meal / food...
16. Your first ever memory...
17. The lesson / subject you like best in school...
18. The lesson / subject you like least in school...
19. Your favourite game or sport...
20. A hobby you enjoy...
21. The hobby you would most like to have...
22. If you had one wish it would be...
23. A good deed you once did...
24. The pet you would most like to have...
25. The animal you are most afraid of...
26. The best ever teacher you had...
27. The best ever birthday you had...
28. The thing you most hate having to do...
29. The thing you are most afraid of...
30. Two nice things about your family...
31. Two nice things about your home...
32. Two nice things about your school...
33. Your favourite story / fairy story...
34. A new ending to X (name a well-known story)...
35. If you ruled the world...
36. The cleverest person you ever met...
37. What this school most needs...
38. If kids ran the school...
39. A time in history you would like to visit...
40. A country you would especially like to visit...
41. If you were invisible...
42. If you could work magic...
43. If you could fly...
44. The day you grew as high as a...
45. The day you shrank as small as a...

Chapter 11 – Managing and Maintaining Talk:Write

It is recommended that each school has a named member of staff who is the leader for Talk:Write. Ideally, this member of staff would have some influence with staff – possibly being a member of senior or middle management already, or someone ready for responsibility. This person would have a passion for quality children's talk and writing and a commitment to Talk:Write.

The Talk:Write leader supports year team leaders and phase leaders in the implementation of the programme through sharing ideas and successes, observation, and the spreading of effective practice.

Talk:Write should be considered a change in approach to the culture of talk in school and the value of extended writing. It is very important, therefore, that routines are established so that, as children move from class to class and year to year, the routines and processes are the same or almost the same.

Some schools may run a trial in one or more years where teachers are confident and eager to institute a new approach to significantly improve talk and writing in their classes. It is helpful to have at least two classes in the trial, so that the teachers involved can consult each other and share ideas and successes. The trial would not normally last more than a term and staff will be updated on its progress and impact in staff meetings and share some of the successes.

When introducing Talk:Write across a whole school for the first time, a trial period should be identified for everyone and made known to all. The focus for the trial might be limited to different parts of the Talk:Write process, with one year focusing most strongly on the work done across the codes of speech and another focusing on the suave writing sessions. Staff should be advised that feedback will be sought from every class teacher on all the aspects of Talk:Write that have been implemented.

This feedback might include news of implementation of any or all of the following:

- The five codes of speech (or as many as the school agrees to discuss).
- The five suave features of language.
- The five 'S' system for spelling of complex suave words.
- The suave writing session.
- The response of pupils to the changes to the room for atmosphere and the special tools for writing.
- The suave word of the week homework and its impact at home and in usage.

- The suave writing homework the night before the suave writing session.
- The development of emergent writer's voice.
- The ability of children to sustain stamina during extended writing.
- The effect on pupils new to English.

Feedback could be collected by year team or phase team leaders during a meeting, which may also provide opportunity for useful discussion. This could then be passed to the Talk:Write leader for collation. The outcomes should be fed back to senior leaders and presented positively at a whole staff meeting, with good examples shared. If needed, the period of induction should then be extended to enable more staff to embed the good feedback received from others.

Once the Talk:Write process is established across the school, it is very important that staff work together, share ideas, and celebrate successes. Towards the end of each term (or twice a year), it is recommended that class teachers complete a targeted assessment for one week's unsupported, extended writing, using the school's own assessment system or the *Oxford Writing Criterion Scale* (Oxford University Press). Progress for each child is tracked on simple spreadsheets that are kept in the class records, with copies of the writing in the Talk:Write leader's records and / or the school's records.

Assessment and tracking is used to target children in need of intervention, and to plan and institute programmes to address areas of slower progress. Tracking systems are used to help identify classes where the programme is most effective for use as models for teachers new to the school, and classes where further support is needed.

It is important to keep discussion on the progress shown in children's writing well to the fore, and good examples should be shared regularly with staff in meetings and with the children in assemblies. This behaviour will encourage all staff to want to share in the success, enthusing them to embrace the programme fully.

If the school launched the programme through the Talk:Write videos, these should remain freely available to members of staff who feel they would benefit from re-watching a section again. Alternatively, the whole staff could refresh through re-watching together six months to a year after the launch. It is not uncommon for some small but important aspects to be omitted when setting up a programme for the first time. If any school is struggling to interpret an aspect of the programme, possibly because of the composition of their pupil body or because they want to use it alongside another programme that they are already committed to, they can contact us for further support and advice.

Working together with other schools who are implementing Talk:Write can be a strength and an asset to all. Best practice can be shared between the schools, and opportunities can be created for staff to visit and observe lessons between the schools. It is most helpful to implement moderation sessions for assessment of writing across families of schools, to ensure consistency of judgements and a sharing of common aspirations for children's performances across the locality.

Talk:Write leaders should visit the website regularly to keep abreast of new resources and materials, which are being generated all the time. These should be shared with staff as soon as is feasible. Termly meetings between the Talk:Write leaders are most useful, especially if they are organised for after the termly assessments and data have been completed. Leaders can exchange outcomes and discuss strengths and areas for further development.

Pupils' achievements should be celebrated in as many ways as is possible. These might include:

- Assemblies.
- Displays.
- Parents' evenings.
- Celebrations.
- School website.
- School magazine.
- Social media.

Above all, Talk:Write leaders should ensure that the driving principles of all children experiencing fun and enjoyment as they grow and develop as talkers and writers are kept to the forefront across all classes in their schools.

As leaders and visitors move around the school, they should be aware of a steady hum of discussion and debate in almost all teaching areas. When they pause to listen, they should hear children mainly talking in Standard English, often with suave features of language that give their speech style and individuality. Discussion with children will show a willingness and ability to identify and use the five codes of speech, code switching for exemplification with ease and enjoyment.

This culture of confidence in use of language will be reflected in children's enthusiasm to speak formally in presentations and performances, and in their writing which will be mature, comprehensive, and enriched with linguistic detail and description when appropriate.

These behaviours will demonstrate that this school is a Talk:Write school!

Summary

Producing confident and articulate talkers who present and discuss in fluent Standard English is an aspiration for all schools, and Talk:Write enables all schools, including those with pupils from diverse backgrounds and communities, to achieve this aspiration. Equally, quality, unsupported writing is a highly complex process that impacts on an individual's success throughout their educational life, in so many ways and across so many subjects.

In the early 2000s, I made a study of the impact of a pupil's skills as a writer on markers and also on the consistency of the quality of English that students brought to their writing of answers in different subjects at GCSE level (15 to 16-year-olds). Many markers confirmed that the first impression of a pupil's ability to write (the neatness of handwriting and the accuracy of the basic skills) influenced their initial opinion as to the pupil's subject knowledge in that subject. This could then influence the marking process.

Through examining marked papers in different subjects, we found that responses on written papers could vary greatly from subject to subject for the same pupil. The largest gap that we detected was a 60 percent difference for the same person between their score on the written paper for English and the written paper for physical education.

The mental impact on an examination marker of a piece of writing that is beautifully expressed and presented is considerable, and frequently influences the marker's receptivity to the writer's subject knowledge. This applies in all aspects of life. A well delivered speech or a well written piece can have enormous impact. Judgements are made from all types of communication and strong talk and writing skills will improve any pupil's life chances. The principles of Talk:Write instil the messages that all presentations in speech and writing are of equal importance and should be of the same high quality.

> Talk:Write provides pupils with a highly enjoyable but effective pathway to becoming articulate communicators and successful writers of the future.

I will leave you with my mantra:

> **When a child can say it, a child can write it.**

Together, we will ensure they can.

Glossary

The 5 Codes of Speech
Standard English, local speak, dialect, suave speak, writer's voice.

The 5 Suave Features of Language
Sophisticated features of writing that include words, sentence openers, connectives, punctuation, and literary features.

The 5 'S' System for Spelling
See, speak, spell, scribe, solve.

Basic Skills
Grammar, handwriting, spelling, and punctuation.

Code Switching
Moving confidently between different codes of speech for different purposes.

Dialect
The unique code of speech that developed historically in isolated communities or that a community develops today, that includes specific vocabulary and grammatical structures.

EAL (English as an Additional Language)
When a speaker of any language other than English learns to speak English.

LDD (Length Through Detail and Description)
Increasing the length of a piece of writing through adding detail and description to various aspects of the writing.

Local Speak
The accent people born and living within a locality may develop that is unique to the locality, both in pronunciation and in shortening of forms.

Orthography
The rules of how a language is represented.

Patois
The unique dialect that develops in a community where the historic language is other than English, but almost all daily communication is now in English. It will include vocabulary and structures that are distinctive to the community.

Phonology
The study of sound patterns and the letters that come together to create the sounds.

Received Pronunciation
A refined accent or form of Standard English often associated with highly educated people, professional people, or people from the south of England.

Stamina with Style
Enabling children to write extended pieces at one sitting while maintaining a good quality of voice and style.

Standard English
Speaking in grammatically correct English, although it may be with a local accent. Writing in grammatically correct forms with accurate spelling and punctuation.

Street Talk
The unique dialect of an inner-city community today, often associated with young people.

Suave Connectives
More sophisticated words and phrases that link or extend sentences – may be adverbs, prepositions, or conjunctions.

Suave It Up
Improving the standard of a piece of writing or inserting more sophisticated features.

Suave Punctuation
The elements of punctuation that enhance flow or impact in writing.

Suave Sentence Openers
The use of varied and impactful strategies to start sentences.

Suave Speak
Speaking in Standard English with sophisticated features of language included.

Suave Word Homework
Weekly whole phase or school homework that introduces a new suave word and promotes discussion and usage within the family.

Suave Words
Sophisticated or ambitious words for the age of the child.

Suave Writing Homework
Discussion with family members the night before the suave writing session, to explore thoughts and ideas related to the stimulus.

Suave Writing Session
The weekly extended, silent writing session.

Writer's Voice
The unique voice and style of a writer (usually published).

References

- Beveridge, L. and Lieschke, J. (2017). *Let's Look at Spelling.*
- Dale and O'Rourke. (1986). *Vocabulary Building.*
- Hart and Risley. (1995). *Meaningful Differences in the Everyday Lives of Young American Children.*
- Hart and Risley. (2003). *The Early Catastrophe: The 30 Million Word Gap by Age 3.*
- Hernik, J. and Jaworska, E. (2018). *The Effect of Enjoyment on Learning.*
- Hirsch Jr, E.D. (2008). *Reading Comprehension Requires Knowledge of Words and the World – Scientific Insights into the Fourth-Grade Slump and the Nation's Stagnant Comprehension Scores.*
- Gabrieli, J. (2018). *Psychological Studies.*
- McKeown, Beck, Omanson, and Pople. (1985). *Some Effects of the Nature and Frequency of Vocabulary Instruction on the Knowledge of Use of Words.*
- Miller, G. A. (1968). *The Psychology of Communication.*
- Oxford University Press. (2021). *Why Closing the Word Gap Matters.*
- Ricketts, Dawson, and Davies. (2021). *The Hidden Depths of New Word Knowledge: Using graded measures of orthographic and semantic learning to measure vocabulary acquisition.*
- Sedita, J. (2020). *The Role of Orthographic Mapping in Learning to Read.*
- Sherrington, T. (2019). *Great CPD. Poor CPD. What are the Signs?*
- Sperry, D. et al. (2018). *Re-examining the Verbal Environments of Children From Different Socio-economic Backgrounds.*
- Trafton, A. (2018). *The Power of Talking with Children.*
- Willis, J. (2007). *The Neuroscience of Joyful Education.*
- Wilson, R. (2015). *Oxford Primary Writing Assessment.*
- Ward, C. M. (2020). *What Are Normal Attention Spans for Children?*

Acknowledgements

- Beth Bennet, recently retired teacher / SENDCo / DHT.
- Simon Blower, Co-Founder, Pobble.
- Alex Crump, Illustrator of *Bonkers Boris Meets the Mayor*.
- Chris Dyson, Headteacher, Parklands Primary School.
- Ben Harding, Independent Education Consultant, Creator of WWNumbers.
- Simon Kidwell, Principal, Trade Union Official.
- Julie Lilly, Headteacher (retired), Manager of Beyond Levels CPD.
- Kirstie Pilmer, Upton Primary School.
- Olympia Publishers, Publishers of *Bonkers Boris Meets the Mayor*.
- Professor Dame Alison Peacock, Chief Executive of the Chartered College of Teaching.
- Professor Sam Twiselton, OBE, Director of Sheffield Institute of Education at Sheffield Hallam University.
- Jez Smith, Lead Professional for English, Discovery Schools Trust.
- Ruth Swailes, School Improvement Advisor, Education Consultant, Curriculum Developer.
- Dawn Titus, Headteacher, St Joseph's Primary School.
- Emma Turner, Research and CPD Lead, Discovery Schools Trust.